WHERE TOLL ROADS MEET

Anthony Holten

ISBN: 978-1-905451-76-0

A CIP catalogue for this book is available from the National Library.

First published in 2008 in co-operation with
Choice Publishing, Drogheda, Co Louth, Ireland
Tel: 041 9841551 Email: info@choicepublishing.ie
Web: www.choicepublishing.ie

WHERE TOLL ROADS MEET

*Exploring the Road Network Around Tara from
Olden Times to the Current M3 Controversy*

Anthony Holten

Contents

Author's Note and Acknowledgements

In this work the various routes of the Dublin to Navan turnpike road have been discussed and analysed, section by section. As there was nobody still living of whom I could ask certain relevant questions, I have been forced to hypothesise somewhat in places. However, any of the surmises I make from time to time are generally based on sound local knowledge, discussion with others and solid research.

I wish to sincerely thank the following people for the assistance they provided in putting together these writings of the area, which is undergoing tremendous change in these times of great progress:

- The staff in Navan Library, especially Frances Tallon of the local history section, who introduced me to Larkin's Map, without which it would have been next to impossible to disentangle some of the mysteries of the past.

- The staff at the National Library, the Ordnance Survey and some of the staff in the NRA in Navan.

- Local historians Michael O'Brien of Johnstown, Mick Kenny of Dunshaughlin, Michael Slavin of Tara, and Liam McCarthy of Garlagh Cross, all of whom provided me with documentation, some old photographs and generously shared their extensive knowledge; and Lydia, the archaeologist in charge of the dig at the

Motte in Dowdstown. And Soo Hee Ding for the photographs of Kilcarn Bridge and the Tollhouse.

- The following people who provided me with much anecdotal information and many clues that helped me out: Noel Devine, Don and Elizabeth (Teeny) O'Brien, Colm Powderley, Dodo Flanagan, Tommy Hamil, Brendan Farrelly, Mickey Creighton, Dan and Moira Norton, Brenda Ferris, Christopher Jordan, Nancy Farrelly, the late Ita Maguire, Jimmy Foley, Greg Murray, Barney Mohan, Malachy Oakes, Mickey Morris, the late Michael O'Brien of Kilcarn, John Bradley, Paddy Daly, the late Maureen Fox, Stephen Ball, the Rev Fr Holloway, Sister Rose D. King, Ger Clarke, Donal Bradley, my brother Tom and his wife Pauline. Also my sisters Breda, Kay and Margaret and my cousin Mairead for all their kindness and help.

- John Long of Co. Tipperary for all his help and encouragement.

- To my wife Marie, my son Joseph, and my daughter Anna-Marie for their time and patience.

- Special thanks to my son John for editing and designing the book and for his help with publishing it.

- And last but not least my mother and father, who passed down the folklore of the area around Kilcarn and Dowdstown, which gave me many clues and filled my childhood mind with an insatiable curiosity and a desire to discover more.

An Introduction

I was born in Dowdstown in 1945 – in a 'tied house' on the Dowdstown estate, just to the north of the Hill of Tara in County Meath. My father worked as a herd for the Columban fathers in Dalgan Park. Our home was in the valley of the River Skane (Skein), the house being located just west of Dowdstown Bridge, where the Skane and the little River Gabhra commingled and flowed on through the Dowdstown estate to join with the River Boyne at the big bend near Ardsallagh.

From my very early years I was aware that an ancient road had once passed through the valley, running directly across the flat plain from the direction of the Hill of Tara and up to the banks of the Skane (Skein) near Dowdstown Bridge. Its remains were plain for all to see then, as it had run on a raised embankment, or causeway, from the south bank of the Skane at the bottom of Cook's garden, it ran all the way across the river field (or gravel hole field) and disappeared into the corner of Barney Norton's farm. On its way it passed by the clump wood and an old nettle and briar covered ruin located beside the wood to the west, finally disappearing at the wet ditch forming the Mearing between Dowdstown and the old parish of Tara at the Clooneen Wood. This was the remains of the Dublin to Navan turnpike road and all the old folk knew it as such, some of them even called it 'the rocky road to Dublin'.

Throughout my youth I often passed along the embankment, sometimes to bring home our cow Betsy for milking and at other times we played hurling and chased elusive corncrakes and grasshoppers in the adjoining meadows. Oftentimes, on our way to play on he Hill of Tara, we ran along the track of the ancient road, crossed into Norton's field and climbed the rusty iron gate leading to the Tara Lane at the corner between the old Clooneen Wood and the 'Teacher's Cottage'. During the great flood of 1954, the entire valley was inundated by floodwaters from the Skane and Gabhra; I have an abiding memory of the causeway being the only piece of dry land in that part of the valley. In my minds eye, I can still see the strip of dry land running across the river field – standing out above the floodwaters and pointing like an arrow straight at the Hill of Tara.

Since my far off childhood in he late 1940s and 1950s, everything has changed utterly. The clump wood was cut down and bulldozed in 1971. Sometime since, the embankment has disappeared, nobody seems to know when or how, some folk even suggest it never existed except in my imagination – but I know differently and I remember it clearly with the yellow furze bushes growing in places along its western edge. Now, the coming of the M3 motorway will obliterate any of the remaining traces of how things were during our young days in that once beautiful valley. The remains of the Clooneen have been bulldozed and replaced by a large sewerage plant, and no doubt more development will follow, it's almost inevitable with progress.

In an attempt to preserve a few of my memories for posterity and perhaps kindle some interest in the past, I have researched the routing and some of the history of the road network in this once beautiful and historic area of County Meath. Not the ancient and medieval history, which has been more than adequately covered by historians and people much more knowledgeable than myself. No, this is a little trip down memory lane, or should I say memories by-roads – from about 1730 to the present day, tracing the exact route of parts of the lost roads and showing where they differ from the present day. I also relate some anecdotes of the areas and mention several significant events, which occurred over the years along the route of this famous road. Nowadays it has evolved into the N3, and it is one of the busiest and most controversial roads in Irish history. This is just my little effort to pass on some of the knowledge I was fortunate enough to acquire at my father's knee – in those far off days before the 'time famine' of the present day engulfed us all. In the era when old folk found time to talk to the children and relate the tales and anecdotes, which they in turn had learned in their own youth.

My main intent in this writing is to establish and record the exact route of the roads and some of the many items of both historical and general interest now lying hidden or perhaps buried alongside these routes – in so far as it's possible to do so, due to all the changes which have occurred over many years. During my own lifetime the alterations in the area have been remarkable, but at least some traces remained to show where the roads once ran in olden times. Also, folk memories were still strong then. Now, with the coming of the motorways and other massive developments, the story is totally different. Whereas in the past, the roads tended to merge with the terrain, generally following the curvature of the hills and valleys – nowadays, our roadbuilders tend to cut great swathes right through the hills and straddle the valleys with huge concrete monstrosities they call bridges, in total disregard to pastoral aesthetics. A vulgar display of raw and unfettered power scarring the landscape forever, it would seem that the prevailing attitude at time of writing is: "we will do so because we can and to hell with the future". Now a new euphenism for modern day vandalism has been coined, namely "preserving by record" – in other words, take a picture of what might once nave been considered a national monument and then bury it under the development. In the future, if people wish to see what the countryside looked like in older times, they will be obliged to visit a museum or an interpretative centre somewhere – what a horrifying prospect. In my youth, we could walk or cycle along the roads and explore the fields and woodlands to see for ourselves – or perhaps ask some of the older generation, altogether a much more pleasant way of doing things. This is my simple effort at preserving some of what were very happy memories and passing on the benefits of my extensive research.

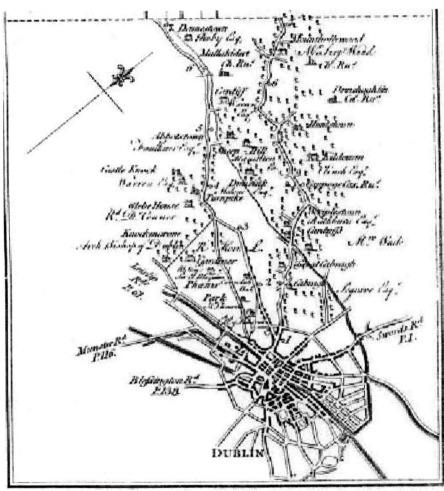

The Taylor/Skinner Map of 1778: From a sequence of the first proper road maps made of Ireland. This section covers the turnpike road from Stoneybatter to Abbotstown (Blanchardstown). The milestones are shown on these maps, number one being located at Stoneybatter.

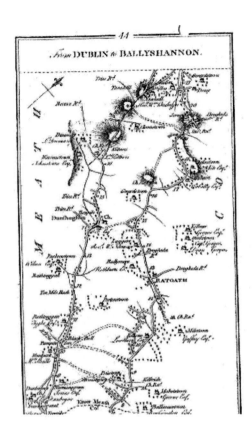

The Taylor/Skinner Map of 1778: From a sequence of the first proper road maps made of Ireland. The map on the left shows the turnpike road from Clonee to Tara and, on the right, from Castletown Cross to Navan.

Chapter 1

The Dublin to Navan Turnpike Road –
Background and History

The above named road originally ran from Stoneybatter, on the north side of Dublin City, close to where the old cattle market was located in later years and terminated at the milestone in Canon, or Cannon Row in Navan. Its end point was marked by this stone, which is now milestone number 23 (formerly number 24) and indicates that it's situated nine and a half miles from Dunshaughlin and 22 miles from Stoneybatter (Irish mile equals 2240 yards or 14 statute to 11 Irish miles). The number one milestone was located at the turnpike (tollhouse) in Stoneybatter, hence every numbered stone on the road indicates a distance one mile greater than the actual distance from the first stone. As Stoneybatter is approximately a mile from the city centre, perhaps this explains the reasoning for such a numbering system? The decision to install milestones at intervals of one Irish mile along the road was made at a road trustees meeting in Navan in 1733.

The section of the road from Dublin to Navan was but a portion of a much longer highway, being part of the Dublin to Ballyshannon road. This explains why, at the time of writing, there are still some old signposts along the road indicating the distances between these far flung locations – I was puzzled by these signs until I carried out some research, now it all makes some sense.

In the 1730s, the turnpike road was routed as follows: Stoneybatter, Blackhorse Lane, Castleknock, Abbotstown (Blanchardstown), Mulhuddart (Malahidert) Clonee, Dunboyne, Blackbull, (here it linked with the Trim to Athboy turnpike road) Dunshaughlin, Killeen, Belper (Ballyna), the hill of Tara, Castletown, Dowdstown, Kilcarn Bridge, the old road, Swan Hill, Butterstream, Ludlow Street, Trimgate Street and Canon Row. It ended at Bannon's Crossroads on the Kells road (at the bottom of the Bohereen Keel (Caol). From here it carried onwards as the Navan to Kells turnpike road – the toll gate (turnpike) for the Kells section was located near where O'Growney's terrace now stands. The milestones continued onwards, with the next stone being sited near Liscarton and numbered 25. The Dublin to Navan turnpike road was the second such Irish road to be approved by Parliament – the first being the route from Dublin to Kilcullen Bridge in County Kildare, they were both approved in 1729. The term turnpike means a gate across a road to stop traffic, so that a toll or levy could be collected. I'm told that the original barriers rotated around a central axis and had tapered metal rings of varying sizes, which made them appear rather like a pike, hence the name. In later days, I believe that some of the barriers consisted of an ordinary pole with a board attached – this could be retracted to allow traffic to pass when the fee was paid.

Imagine a young engineer standing on top of the little knoll, which in my younger days was known as Barry's Hill and was located on the Dublin side of Kilcarn Bridge on the old route of the road. This young man had been commissioned to build a Coachroad from Navan to Dublin and he was standing on the hilltop in the year 1725 or thereabouts. The reason why he stood in that particular place being that the old bridge at Kilcarn was the only 'dry' Boyne crossing on his prospective route to the far off city of Dublin. The big bend in the River Boyne at Ardsallagh prevented him from using a route to the west of the river, as Bellinter Bridge had not yet been built and would not be in existence until the elapse of nearly a hundred more years. Now, as he gazed across the green countryside towards the city, he was faced with a choice – to his left was a relatively flat route across rolling hills, this was a fairly obvious choice, as to his right and blocking his route lay the Hill of Tara. Though it wasn't a very high hill, being somewhat less than five hundred feet, hence it was by no means an insurmountable obstacle. In those days no bulldozers or other earthmoving equipment of any sort existed, except men with spades, shovels and pickaxes, therefore the roads of the day tended to follow the contours of the terrain and not plough through everything like nowadays.

Yet the route across the hill was chosen. Why did the engineers of the day choose to build the turnpike road across the Hill of Tara and put all that extra load on the horses – pulling the big coaches up the steep 'slope of the chariots', to surmount the ancient hill? The answer of course is fairly obvious, as the question is partly rhetorical in the first place. There must have been an existing road running across Tara and this might only require upgrading to make it more suitable for the coaches. The old road across the hill may have consisted of portions of several of the

legendary five roads of Tara, possibly parts of the *Slighe Cualann,*
Slighe Dhala and the *Slighe Asail* – with the routes of the day
evolving from the ancient *Slighte* during the intervening years.

Over many years there has been much divergence of opinion
amongst the great scholars as to whether these ancient roads
actually converged on Tara or on Dublin. But if they first appeared
in a dream on the night of the birth of 'Conn of the hundred
battles', in AD 123, as stated in the 'Annals of the Four Masters' –
or were purpose built to repel a threatened Roman invasion, as
believed by Peter O Keefe, matters not a whit to my story of the
turnpike road. Being born and reared in the locality and brought up
on the ancient legends of Tara, I would tend towards the belief that
the *Slighte* once converged on Tara – though indeed there could
be an element of truth in both schools of thought. Whatever the
truth of the matter, I think we will never know for sure now, as too
much time has elapsed since those days. This is another reason
why I believe we should record what we do know, whilst it can
mostly be verified.

Research has shown that the present route of the N3, from
Dunshaughlin to Philpotstown Cross (Garlow Cross) came into
existence about sixty years later, in 1796 – 1798. At the time of the
rebellion in 1798, both the new line of the turnpike from
Dunshaughlin to Philpotstown and the old line through Killeen and
across the Hill of Tara were probably still open concurrently. Much
of the action during the rebellion in County Meath took place along
these sections of the turnpike road – culminating in the Battle of
Tara on the 26th of May of that year. The rebels were routed by
Loyalist troops who marched along the old road from

Dunshaughlin through Killeen and no doubt many of the defeated Croppies fled along the road. This defeat, which occurred alongside the old turnpike road, signalled the collapse of the rebellion in the area and the subduing of the freedom fight for many years – so from this perspective alone, the old road is indeed historic.

During his research, Peter O Keefe discovered that the Mail Coach Road map of the turnpike, covering the section between the Blackbull and Navan, has disappeared, or perhaps it never existed. Hence there is no coherent record of this part of the actual route, except what can be gleaned from other maps and writings and interested individuals with some local knowledge. However I'm digressing somewhat, I'm starting in the middle of the story so to speak, but I felt that it was necessary to explain why it was decided to build the road over the highest hill in the area – rather than the easier and flatter route chosen in later years.

Finally, the main purpose of these writings, as previously stated, is not to depict the lifestyle of the people of the era or the many types of conveyances on the roads at the time – nor indeed the types of roads or their methods of construction. These aspects of the Irish road network are already well covered in some excellent books. My main purpose is to establish the exact routes, in olden times, of some of the roads in this very interesting and historic area. Many of the old routes are known anecdotally and the knowledge has passed down through the generations – but some have merged back into the landscape, with only an odd ditch or perhaps the ruins of an old bridge or habitation to indicate their former presence and for the curious to ponder over. Others have metamorphosed into modern roads and are still being driven upon today, with most of the travellers thereon not knowing the history of the route – some not giving a hoot either, their overwhelming desire being to get to the other end of the road in the shortest possible time. For others who are curious about such things and wonder why such and such a peculiar bend or ditch is there on a particular road, perhaps this information will be of some interest? With the passing of our generation, I feel that it's the end of a particular era, people tend to be much more mobile nowadays and hence the acquisition of local knowledge is more difficult. Therefore, I feel that we owe it to future generations to pass on any such knowledge we have been fortunate enough to glean from previous generations.

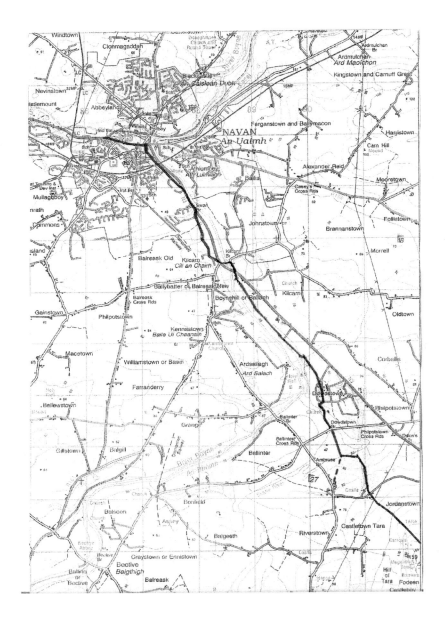

Discovery Map No. 1: Navan to Tara.

The heavy black line denotes the original route of the turnpike road.

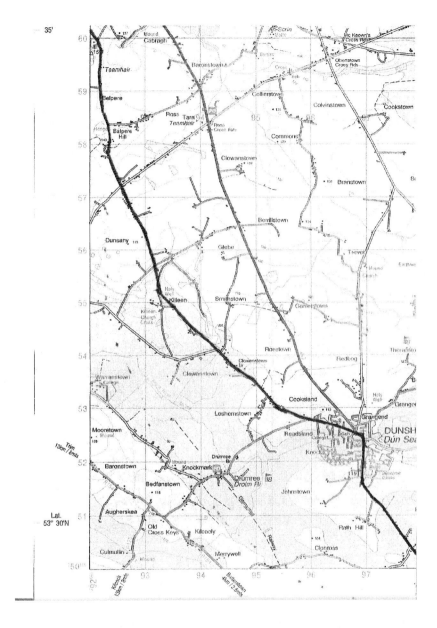

Discovery Map No. 2: Tara to Ballinlough.

The heavy black line denotes the original route of the turnpike road.

Chapter 2

A Journey in Times Past

Let us take a trip on a coach from Bannon's Cross in Navan through the turnpikes at Kilcarn and Dunshaughlin, then onwards to the Blackbull Inn. This is the section of the road that I'm mostly writing about. The year is around 1780 and we are going to travel along the Navan to Dublin turnpike road – from the final milestone at Canon Row to the junction with the Trim/Athboy turnpike road at 'the Blackbull Inn' and "the Flathouse Inn just beyond it near the number 10 milestone at the Pace. We have already made the journey up from Kells on that other section of turnpike and now we're facing the onward journey to Dublin, a distance of twenty-three Irish miles.

Driving up Canon Row (Cannon Row), a narrow street, we pass number 24 milestone, the last numbered stone of the section – this indicated the distance to Dunshaughlin as being ten and a half Irish miles. Turning left at the intersection with the Trim road, which led on up Brewshill (Brews Hill), we headed off down Trimgate Street. On arrival at the "triangular square", we turned down the street to the right (Ludlow Street) and pulled into the Inn on the left. The horses were changed by the hostler and following some refreshments we boarded the big coach and headed out the turnpike road towards Dublin. The road ran close to the River Boyne as we passed the number 23 milestone – this being located just east of the slip leading down to the water. Our next landmark of note was the Swan Bridge, a small stone bridge spanning a little and unnamed stream. Here the road swung to the right, away from the Boyne and up a slight eminence known as Swan Hill. Halfway up the hill we stopped at an Inn named 'the Swan' and the drivers changed. The Inn was a hostelry used mainly by coachmen (or carmen) and the lower orders of travellers in those days. Next we drove on up the hill, passing Balreask, where many soddies and poor dwellings stood by the roadside, then on we went towards the river crossing at Kilcarn Bridge. This famous old bridge spanned the River Boyne west to east, its eleven arches joining the townlands of Ballybatter (the town of the road) and Atlumney (the place of the shallow ford).

Driving down the steep hill we came to Kilcarn turnpike, where the toll was paid – (the decision to open a turnpike at Kilcarn Bridge was made at the road trustees meeting of the 16th of April 1730 and the first tolls were collected on the 10th of May that same year). On payment of the toll, we proceeded across the widened ancient stone arched bridge. Following the river crossing, our road swung sharply to the right and climbed the short steep hill by Kilcarn Lodge. Halfway up the hill was a drinking well with cool clear water pouring over the edge of the stone drinking trough, but we didn't stop there. Beyond the hilltop a stone-built coach house stood on the right, this also had a good spring well down on the steep riverbank. We followed the road on past the mill at Lower Kilcarn (the big mill) – with its stone gabled house close by and set on the riverbank immediately above the long weir. This weir directed the raised level of the river waters into the two millwheels – the tailrace of the mill re-entered the main river downstream of the two easternmost arches of the old bridge at Kilcarn. Proceeding onwards, we drove past the entrance to the estate at Nether Kilcarn or Lower Kilcarn on the left, the property of Barry Esquire – then on past a stone built hostelry on the right and milestone number 22. This stretch of highway was cut into the riverbank and passed through green pastoral landscapes along the beautiful valley of the River Boyne. Here, a big wooded island and the skew built weir athwart the river at Lower Kilcarn slowed the flow of the great river until it appeared to be almost at a standstill, its flow seemingly slow and lifeless.

The next point of note on our journey was the entrance to the estate at Upper Kilcarn, again on our left and also the property of Barry Esquire. This entrance was part of a narrow road leading up to the Oldtown road at Pastor Hill and joined it near to the southernmost Rath. The two estates, Upper and Lower Kilcarn, were linked by an avenue that also joined up with this narrow roadway a short distance up from the turnpike road. About halfway to the Rath, the narrow road up to Oldtown had a junction with the laneway leading past the old Norman Church and graveyard of Kilcarn, which in turn joined the Oldtown road at Crohanboy (Croboy).

Next we drove in to the cobblestoned yard of the mill house at Upper Kilcarn. Reputedly a mill had been located on this site from about the late 1600s, it was a corn mill and was situated at the head of the millrace and close by a quarry on the riverbank.

Here again a great skewed weir bisected the river, from the far bank at Ardsallagh to the tip of the millrace on the Kilcarn side. The low rumble of the water pouring across the weir could be heard from where we sat in the coach in the cobbled yard. This yard contained stables on the side towards the river and a dwelling house on the opposite side. The house was substantial and of stone and mudwall construction, with a thatched roof and the door opened out onto the yard – almost on to the road itself. Some of the coaches used this place as a rest stop and sometimes changed the horses, but our intended stop was further up the road, close by the River Skane in Dowdstown. We didn't tarry, but carried on up the road that passed through the yard and on towards Dowdstown to the south – on the way we drove by a fine well to the right and further on a big limekiln built into the steep banks of the river.

The junction with the Drogheda Road came next, with its tiny hamlet of poor houses clinging to the banks of the nearby Follistown River. This river, though mostly a small stream, could at times of flood become a mighty torrent, hence a stone arched bridge bore the turnpike across the deep cleft. Locals knew this bridge by various names, including, Brian Boru's Bridge and Saint Patrick's Bridge – on the east side of the crossing and to the left of the road, was a rather large quarry, which supplied limestone to the nearby kiln. The river was a very important landmark, forming the boundary between parishes and townlands, including those of Dowdstown and Kilcarn.

Shortly after the river crossing, we passed a small laneway on the right, it was cut through the wooded bluffs overlooking the

Boyne meadows. The steep banks were covered by a myriad of wild flowers and strawberry plants, providing a very colourful sight indeed for the eyes of the weary traveller. The little laneway led down to the shallow ford on the River Boyne at Ardsallagh, just beside a holy well on the western banks of the river. The spring was known as Saint Brigid's well and was very old, some say it could possibly date back to the monastery supposedly located in Ardsallagh in the 6th century.

We were now driving through some wooded terrain and the fine parklands of the Taylor Estate in Dowdstown. The road ran down past milestone number 21, then on by Dowdstown House, standing on our right. The house was a solid two storied stone structure, build in the cottage style, with a large walled-in courtyard to the rear and a stone coach house to the side. It was situated on a flat bench of parkland, overlooking the dramatic view across the 'big bend' in the River Boyne, which at this point turned almost 90 degrees to the west. The magnificent view being enhanced by the haw-haw running from near the river and almost up to the house, thereby allowing an unobstructed view across the fields to the river and the high grounds of Ardsallagh beyond.

Passing the walled garden to our left, we drove on up the winding turnpike to the top of Dowdstown Hill – now we had a panoramic view over the valleys of the Skane and the Boyne, with the woods of Bellinter and Ardsallagh providing a green canopied background. Our road, previously heading west, now swung to the south again as we commenced the steep and winding descent of the hill – on the way downhill a magnificent view of the Hill of Tara unfolded directly to the south. We passed the ruins of Dowdstown

Church, built by Sir Walter Duff, a Norman knight, around 1180 and came to a fork in the road, just below the ancient churchyard. At this place, the other Dublin to Navan road, routed via Ratoath and Skryne, joined up with the Navan to Dublin turnpike, routed via Tara and Dunshaughlin.

Now we drove along the realigned road, over an embankment crossing the swampy valley and then traversed the River Skane by a stone arched bridge. Off to the left we could see the original route through the valley. It skirted to the east of the swampy hollow, passed by Tobair Na Mias (the well of the dishes), then swung back to the west again – crossing the little River Gabhra by means of an old wooden bridge and rejoined the turnpike over towards the Clooneen Wood. We drove through the forked junction with the Trim road, a narrow track leading off to our right towards Bellinter and Bective. Then the Skane was re-crossed by means of a humped backed stone bridge close by its confluence with the Gabhra, this bridge took the turnpike road up onto a raised embankment, or causeway, near the south end of which was the hostelry. Here we stopped to change the horses and to provide a brief interlude for the passengers.

Following our brief halt our journey was resumed – the passengers refreshed and the horses changed for the long hard pull lying ahead. The embankment, though much lower, continued until we came to the steep hill of the Clooneen Wood (this name translates to "the wood of the little meadow") – it was a fine copse of about ten acres of beech, chestnut and oak trees. At this spot the highway forked – the road to the right continued up the steep ridge and on through the wood towards Kilmessan. Whilst the turnpike, on which we were travelling, swung sharply to the left, now heading eastwards across the slope. Following the sharp turning, we crossed a small stone Kesh spanning a little streamlet, flowing briskly and tumbling down a small waterfall towards the River Gabhra, which meandered but a stones throw away to our left. Near the Kesh, a laneway led down towards a thatched corn mill nestling at the junction of the Gabhra and the small stream. Several buildings surrounded the mill, one of which seemed to be a rather large stone granary or grange. The whole area being a charming spot, almost an enchanted place, with the pink flowered chestnut trees of the Clooneen, the blossoming hawthorns and the flower covered banks of the roadside ditches providing a colourful display for the eye, whilst the tinkling of the brook and waterfall made a musical accompaniment.

Shortly thereafter, at a farmhouse or some such small dwelling, the road swung sharply to the right and headed directly towards Tara again – here we passed milestone number 20 and the gradual ascent of the hill began. We climbed up the steepening rise until the gradient levelled off as we approached a crossroads. The crossroads was known as Castletown Cross and named after the townland we were passing through – this in turn derived its name from a nearby castle, the ruins of which we could see standing behind a farmhouse close by the turnpike and to our right. Supposedly, the former owner of the towerhouse was a prominent Jacobite named Cheevers, who had fought against King Billy at the Battle of the Boyne in 1690 and had been dispossessed, for his pains. Passing through the crossroads we commenced climbing again, the incline gradually growing steeper as we climbed ever nearer the famous hilltop. Now we were ascending a section of the road known to scholars and historians as 'the slope of the chariots', supposedly in ancient times, the warriors of the High Kings of Tara once raced their chariots on these slopes. Some say the turnpike road here was built over one of the five ancient roads of Tara, perhaps the *Slige Asail* or the *Slige Cualann,* but who shall ever know the truth of such matters?

Passing the number 19 milestone, we reached the summit of the road and beheld a breathtaking vista – the view from the hilltop is famous, some people say they have seen landmarks in eleven counties. On a clear day, one can see from the Slieve Bloom Mountains in County Laois to the far off Mourne Mountains in County Down. But we had no time to tarry, we passed the road leading down to Lismullin and the Decoy beyond – then the village of Taragh on our left, with the small thatched Inn sitting snugly into the hillside to the right of the road. Carrying on southwards, we saw Saint Patrick's well to the right, with its little outflowing stream forming a drinking pool by the roadside, locals knew this place as the Haw-Haw. The small stream ran under the road and disappeared down towards Newhall, finally mingling with the Gabhra in the Lismullin estate to the east.

Leaving the famed hilltop, the coach drove on down the southern slope of the hill, which was much less steep and the descent more gradual. We passed a little road to the right, leading to the site of the ancient Monastery and castle at Odder and onwards to Kilmessan, Bective (Ballyna) and Trim. Next, the mound of Rathmaeve loomed to our right, with the road to Skryne directly opposite, this area was known as Belper. Milestone number 18 was located just past the Skryne road junction. Shortly thereafter we came to Ballyna crossroads, where the turnpike crossed over the main road from Trim to Drogheda, with the village of Dunsany a short distance off to the right. Having climbed the hill from the crossroads, we came to another hostelry where we stopped for refreshment and a change of horses following the long pull up Tara. The area was renowned for highwaymen, but on the day we saw none and after this brief interlude in our journey we proceeded onwards without being held up.

Continuing southwards, we passed milestone number 17 and crossed the narrow Killeen road – at the eastern end of this road was the townland of Birrelstown, near the Glebe, whilst to the west it led on to the Dunsany to Dunshaughlin road. Now we drove on through the wooded Demesne of Killeen Castle, the grounds of the estate stretched into the distance, open green parklands interspersed with some cultivated fields and many spinneys and copses, all very pleasing to the eye of the traveller. We drove on past where a waterfall tumbled into a pond and the renowned holy well, known as Ladywell. Though the turnpike wound its way quite close to the old Norman castle, yet we couldn't see much of the building itself – the occasional glimpses of its many towers peeking through the shielding trees being the only tangible proof that there was indeed a castle there. Passing the ancient church, or oratory and exiting the Killeen estate at a place later named the "green gates"; we joined the main road from Kilmessan to Dunshaughlin at Clavinstown Bridge. Having crossed the bridge over a tiny tributary of the Skane, we came upon a small road leading off to the left. This was the road to the Glebe and it ran back towards

Birrelstown – near the junction we could see Clavinstown Mill, a big multistorey stone building with many doors and windows. The overshot waterwheel was driven by the small tributary river over which we had just crossed.

Driving on towards Dunshaughlin, we saw another mill beyond milestone number 16. The mill, set in a little secluded valley to the right of the road (Devlin's Mill), was being driven by the waters of yet another small tributary of the Skane. Then we passed a narrow lane leading to the south and on to the Drumree road. Further on was milestone number 15, a few perches before the turnpike joined with the road from Drumree and Trim. – the coach was on the last leg of the journey to Dunshaughlin.

At the entrance to the village, we stopped at the turnpike tollhouse, this being a small house at the roadside, where a pole barrier blocked the highway. When the driver paid his dues, the pole was withdrawn through a hole in the wall and the coach proceeded up the village street, where we stopped at yet another hostelry, the Fingal Arms. Here the horses were watered and fed oats and vetches, but not changed, the passengers partaking of some light refreshments. Then we proceeded on through the village, passing near the source of the River Skane; at this spot it was a mere streamlet, which rose in a nearby well close to the mainstreet. Towards the far end of the village, the coach drove on by number 14 milestone. As we headed on southwards towards Rathbeggan the number 13 milestone was passed at Parsonstown. Then we came upon number 12 milestone shortly before arriving at a small village named 'the Ten Mile Bush'. When or how the latter place received such a name I have no idea, but it's a very old name and was already called such when the Taylor and Skinner map was surveyed in the 1770s. I had seen it marked as such when I perused the map before setting out on my journey. As it doesn't seem to be ten miles distance from any place of great noteworthiness – except Kilcarn Bridge, perhaps this is the explanation? Shortly after passing Rathbeggan crossroads, number 11 milestone was left in our wake – we were approaching the end of our journey at Blackbull Inn and the number 10 milestone just beyond. 'The Flathouse', another Inn, was located at the nearby Woodpark Crossroads. According to the Taylor and Skinner map, the Inn is on the borders of an area with the rather unusual name of 'Great Pace'. The Blackbull was a Posting House and Coachman's Inn with some stables attached where horses could be changed. The Inn stood close to the junction of the former turnpike road to Trim and Athboy, which ran westwards and crossed the River Tolka via a triple arched stone bridge named 'the Blackbull Bridge. The road was no longer a turnpike and the old tollhouse on the corner was now a habitat for some local family. The Trim to Athboy turnpike road act was passed in Parliament in 1731, but in 1752, Parliament failed to enable the act again, therefore it lapsed and the tollhouse here had closed down long since. Thus, the road from the Blackbull to Athboy was the first turnpike road in Ireland to be discontinued as a toll-road – having existed as such for just twenty-one years. The Flathouse Inn was a much larger establishment, which straddled the junction of the road leading eastwards. As it was getting late, I decided to avail of the hospitality of the Inn and continue the onward journey to Dublin on the morrow. So ended this stage of my journey on the

Navan to Dublin turnpike toll road.

As the reader most likely guessed, this journey was fictitious, merely a product of my imagination. But it is based on the actual old route of the said turnpike road and a great deal of research. I have studied many documents, books and maps and much of the evidence can be deduced from these – but the missing link was provided by my youthful memories of the remains of the old road running close by my home in Dowdstown all those years ago. It passed through my childhood playpen, the fields and woods around Dowdstown and Tara, and its memory left an indelible impression on my psyche. In those early days, when we chased the elusive corncrake and grasshoppers in the meadows adjacent to the ancient embankment and fished for minnows and pinkeens in the Gabhra and the Skane, little did we realise what was to come. The depredation about to be visited upon the area by progress and farming, and, that one day a mighty motorway would be driven through our field of dreams, obliterating all traces of what had once been there – such things were unimaginable to us then.

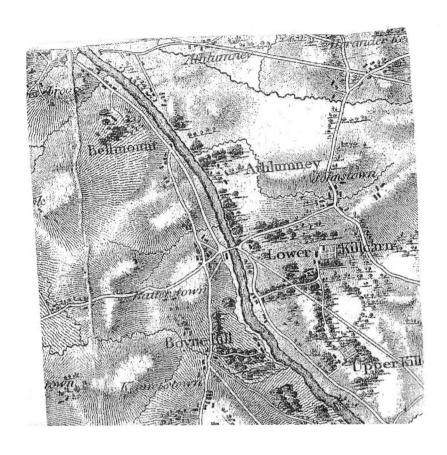

Section of Larkin's Map (1812 – 1817):

The turnpike road from Navan to Kilcarn.

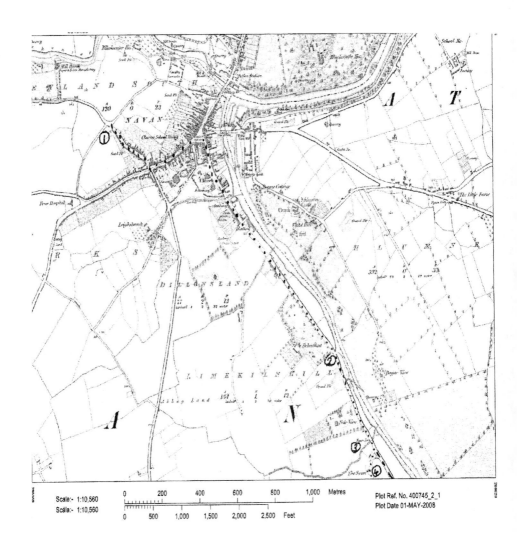

1836 OS Map: Navan to Swan Inn.

... denotes older line of road   – – – denotes newer line of road

1: Bannon's Cross   2: 'The Slip'

3: Swan Bridge   4: Swan Inn

1836 OS Map: Kilcarn.

...   denotes older line of road   – – – denotes newer line of road

5: The Tollhouse.   **6. Kilcarn Mill ('The Big Mill')**

Chapter 3

From Bannon's Cross to Dowdstown via Kilcarn Bridge

This portion of the turnpike is relatively easy to deal with and to understand, as much of the route can still be driven on today – at least at the time of writing in 2007. It covers a distance of just under three Irish miles. The section runs from the present day roundabout at the bottom of the Bohereen Keel (Caol) near Scoil Mhuire, to Brian Boru's Bridge (Saint Patrick's Bridge}, at the edge of the Dowdstown estate, via "the old road" at Balreask and across Kilcarn Bridge. As previously described, the turnpike road started from Bannon's Cross, where the Kells road intersected Abbey Road and the Bohereen Keel, and ran on past the milestone in Canon Row. At time of writing, the stone reads nine and a half miles to Dunshaughlin and is now milestone number 23, but in older days, as shown on the Taylor and Skinner map, it was milestone number 24. The difference in the mileage reflects the shortening of the highway effected by the many realignments of the road over the intervening years.

At the top of Canon Row we come to the intersection with the Trim road, at time of writing it's called Finnerty's Corner, previously being named Glacken's Corner. According to Taylor and Skinners map, the street later named Chapel Lane and now Railway Street, didn't exist then, nor did the present day Trim road. Instead, the old Trim road started at the top of Trimgate Street, and ran up through Brews Hill, then on out the Commons Road. In the past, the old town wall crossed the street beside 'the young mens hall', near Saint Mary's Church – part of its remains were to be found in a pub alongside the hall. The gate in the town wall was most likely located here. Hence the logic of calling it Trimgate Street, as it was the entrance, or gateway, to the Trim road. In my youth, a large portion of the aforementioned town wall once adorned Metge's Lane but in recent times it was demolished to make way for some development work. At time of writing, there's still some of it standing in the Urban Council Yard, in Abbey Road, but no doubt it too will soon bite the dust to make way for some more 'progressive' development!

The Trim road continued out through Shambo Cross and on through Robinstown (Ballbraddagh – 'the thievish town' – John O'Donovan 1836), and on past the 'black road', eventually joining the Trim road near Rathnally, as it does at present.

Market Square, Ludlow Street, the old Courthouse and Thubberorum (Tobar Oran), the Hotel or Inn, the Protestant Church and the County Infirmary were all there then. The site of the Inn later became the Russell Arms Hotel (the Club), this was demolished in recent years and the Newgrange Hotel built in its place. Somebody once told me that there were three Inns in Navan in those early days of the tollroad and that one Inn was known as the Blackbull. The turnpike road continued on down Bridge Street, where it crossed the Leighsbrook, then on through Academy Street and Butterstream (Limekiln Street) and out to the Swan Bridge. It ran pretty much on the same route as the later day N3, until the construction of the inner relief road in the 1970s. On its way it passed by Dillonsland, the slipway to the river at Belmount and the Limekiln Hill. The slipway leading down to the water, was still there in my youth, it was then known as 'the Slip' – I remember it well, directly opposite Spicers Gate Lodge and close to the 'Boiler Mc'Guinness's' house. It's clearly marked on the Ordnance Survey map of 1836, so it's reasonable to suggest that it was there a few years earlier, as the rate of change was much slower then.

Either the Swan Bridge derived its name from the Inn close by, which was named "The Swan", or the Inn was named after the bridge – at this remove I cant ascertain which was which. It doesn't really matter, though the Inn is long gone, the bridge is still there, or at least there's a bridge spanning the stream. The present day road, from Swan Bridge to Kilcarn was constructed much later, probably during one of the many realignments that took place over the years – it starts at a little hill known in my youth as 'the Skelp', more about this anon. In the early days of the turnpike road the route swung to the right here and up the Swan Hill, this section of road became known locally as 'the old road', many of the old timers still call it that today. Then it went on past the Coachman's Inn (The Swan) – this stood on the right hand side of the road as you go up the hill towards Balreask, more or less where the Ardboyne Hotel is situated at present. I recall it well, as several times, in my youth I helped my father to dose cattle in sheds which were formerly the stables. It was an old mud and stone two-storey house and if I recall correctly, it had a slated roof in those days. The sheds backed onto the old tollroad and formed a high stone wall close to the roadside, with big stone piers forming the entrance gateway at the Balreask end. The house and sheds were demolished during the development that took place in later years. For those interested enough, both 'the Swan' and Swan Bridge can be seen clearly on the 1836 OS map. Some people suggest that the name of the hill and the Inn derive from a family named Swan who lived there in the early part of the twentieth century and who leased some land to Navan Rugby Club during its early years. Whilst this may possibly be true, research has shown that the name is much older and, as stated, is shown on the 1836 OS map – it possibly predates this and may be as old as the turnpike road itself.

A short distance past the Inn, a laneway led off to the right – this originally ran across to the old Trim road (the Commons Road nowadays). Some locals knew it as Swan's Lane. Across from this, on the other side of the turnpike road, lay the ruins of an old church and burial grounds – a local anecdote says that the bodies of several Croppies, killed at the battle of Tara in 1798, are interred there and it's known by some locals as the "Croppie's Graveyard".

Next was the junction at Kilcarn. In the days, prior to the advent of the railway, the roads in this area were somewhat different. Just before the descent of the hill leading down to the bridge at Kilcarn, a road cut across to the Cannistown road. It ran along the top of the high ridge above the buildings and joined the latter road somewhere near the junction of the present day Bothar Ailinne (beautiful road), which wasn't in that location then. It was realigned when the railway came in later years. On Larkins Map, the said 'beautiful road' ran across to Gainstown crossroads, where it met the then Trim road. As it is not shown on this map, it would seem to suggest that the present day new line of the Trim road was cut sometime after 1812 and prior to 1836. It is on the OS map and there are several references to 'the new line' of the Trim road in O' Donovan's letters, associated with the survey of that year, specifically in the context of the parish of Bective. Larkin's Map shows that the Cannistown road also cut up the hill, more or less on its present routing. I believe this road was once known as 'the road to the mill', it being the direct road to Kilcarn Mill. The Taylor and Skinner map doesn't show any great detail of the junction at Kilcarn, but it's not important, as I found that, though this map is very useful in tracing the main routes, its accuracy on the secondary roads is somewhat suspect. On the other hand, both the 1836 OS map and Larkin's Map agree on the main features of the roads around Kilcarn. However, there is one very important anomaly in Larkin's Map, which I feel is important to point out – it shows the main buildings to be on the upstream side of the bridge, whereas the OS maps and all local anecdote indicates that they were always in their present position, on the downstream, or Navan side of the bridge.

There was a Smithy at the bottom of the hill, just at the start of the Cannistown road – I remember it well in my youth. In those days, Dad carried me on the bar of his bike as he led Polly, our Cob pony, from our home in Dowdstown, to be shod at the Kilcarn forge. Old Mick Markey was the Blacksmith then, and I recall the shoeing operation very well. In my memory, I can still hear the roar of the bellows and the musical ringing of the hammer on the anvil as I write – whether there was a Smithy there in the times of the coaches and the turnpike road, I just don't know. It is likely that there was, as it was there at the turn of the nineteenth century – there's a building shown on this exact spot on the 1836 OS map. I'm told that Mick Markey's father ran a forge in Ardbracken in older times and that many of the family were skilled Blacksmiths.

But I digress somewhat, so back to the main story, the route of the Dublin to Navan turnpike road in the latter half of the eighteenth century. The fact that the old stone bridge at Kilcarn had been widened (the width of the road was increased) at some time is well known – its original width was thirteen feet six inches, between sidewalls, this being increased to just over eighteen feet road width. If you take a boat and float under the stone arches, the joint in the stonework can be readily seen. A few years ago, sometime in the 1980s, when a portion of the side of the bridge fell in to the river, the joining was plain for all to see from above. But when was the bridge widened? Nobody seems to know for sure – but I would suggest that it's likely it was extended to accommodate the larger coaches when the road was converted to turnpike status around 1730. The Longfield estate map of 1822 showing the Kilcarn Demesne, clearly indicates the ten upstream 'flow splitters', or cutwaters, these are part of the present day structure – therefore the widening of the bridge occurred sometime prior to this date. So it's possible that the increased width of the bridge and the consequent widening of the road occurred around about the time of the inauguration of the turnpike status of the road. Though I have no way of proving this point, yet it seems logical to me.

Supposedly, the original structure contained thirteen eyes, some of these, the central arches, were supposedly much wider than the present day spans. Peter O Keefe considers that the present day bridge dates back to the late 17th or early 18th century. Nobody is certain when the original bridge was built here, but it was possibly sometime in the 13th century, and the historians reckon there was a ford here on the river for many years prior to that. Seemingly this was the main crossing of the Boyne from the earliest times, which lends credence to the stories that the turnpike road is built upon the line of one of the ancient *Slighte.* The bridge links the townland of Ballybatter (the town of the road) on the Navan side of the bridge to Athlumney on the Dublin side – some say Athlumney translates to 'the ford of the bare place' or alternatively to 'the ford of the herds'. I'm told that the original ford of Athlumney was located near Navan and just upstream from the stone built railway viaduct. I recall that the tailrace from Lower Kilcarn mill (the big mill) was once routed through the two easternmost arches – with a dividing rampart taking the millstream all the way down to the bridge. During my lifetime, the rampart collapsed and the old millrace has coalesced with the main river once more.

The lands of both Lower and Upper Kilcarn (or Greater Kilcarn and Little Kilcarn) have long been associated with the Barry family of Santry in County Dublin. A Richard Barry first came into possession of the combined estates around 1630. The Civil Survey of the 1650s indicates a mill at Lower Kilcarn at the time, this mill was known as the big mill. There was no mill shown at Upper Kilcarn (Little Kilcarn) at the time of the survey. The first mention of the smaller corn mill, that I can find, is in 1702, so this mill possibly came into being sometime between the date of the Civil Survey and the latter date.

A few additional points about Kilcarn, and then we'll move on. Most people accept the notion, that the turnpike, or tollhouse, was only located on the Navan side of the bridge, at what is now known as "the Old Bridge Inn, or "the Willows Restaurant" – but I'm not convinced, as I have seen no proof of this assertion. Griffith's valuation of 1854 contains an entry for a tollhouse in the townland of Balreask Old, but this was just prior to the dissolution of the tollroads, which at the time were controlled by the Commissioners of Public Works. The record indicates that the aforesaid Commissioners leased the tollhouse and had an exemption from paying rent. On the Taylor and Skinner map, though the turnpike is shown on the Navan side of the bridge, yet the location is not pinpointed and I have been unable to find any trace of it on any of the other maps. In my opinion, the turnpike was located in several places during its almost one hundred and thirty years existence – I think there are other possible locations where the tolls were collected for a time, these I will explain presently.

On the Johnstown side, the junction seems to have remained unchanged for centuries – until the new bridge was built in the 1970s, and then everything changed utterly and forever. In my youth there were two adjoined houses at the corner of the Johnstown road, the one nearest the bridge being then occupied by Jack Sarsfield, a well known local character. When boarding the bus in Navan, he was often heard telling the driver, "drop me at Swamp Villa", his name for the house by the Boyne, which was frequently flooded. I'm told that the deeds for this house indicated it was once a tollhouse – this sits well with my ideas about the tollhouse being situated on the Dublin side of the bridge for a time and warrants some further investigation in the future. A family named Cuff occupied the adjoined house. These houses are still there, but I heard recently that they're to be knocked and replaced by a block of apartments.

Nowadays, the area is almost unrecognisable, compared to just a few years ago. Kilcarn Lodge, which sits on the high bank on the Johnstown side, was known to us in our youth as Barry's House, because a family named Barry resided there. The hill on the road was known as Barry's Hill, but in former times it was called the Kennel Hill. A pack of hounds being kennelled in the big stone stables and the field to the rear was called the Kennel Field. During World War Two, 'the Emergency', a concrete pillbox was built into the high bank just below the lodge. This is only one of many such 'fortifications' to be found around the bridges over the River Boyne. Quite what they were supposed to be fortifying against I'm at a loss to understand – if either the Germans or the Americans had invaded, a couple of well aimed artillery shells would have made short work of these concrete coffins, which were generally built from poor quality cement and aggregate. During our youth, they provided local children with a great play area. Many unsuspecting motorists were ambushed, both at Kilcarn and Bellinter Bridges, the kids poking their ash plants and hurley sticks, imaginary rifles or bazookas, out through the rifle slits, which at least provided a magnificent view over the famous bridges – being of no use for any other purpose.

There was a spring well built into the high roadside bank, near the gate to Barry's house (Kilcarn Lodge) – this flowed into a stone trough, which overflowed and formed a little stream by the roadside. The water was beautiful and cool to drink, many a time I hopped off my bike to sup the lovely clear liquid on those hot summer days of yesteryear. The older folk told many stories of the horse drawn drays of hay, which stopped here for the horses to be watered on their way to the haymarket in Dublin. Don O Brien from Johnstown told me that as a child, he heard his first football match commentary here in 1927, if he recalls correctly, Meath were playing Kildare. As radios were pretty scarce in the parish in those days, a large crowd of locals had gathered outside the house to listen to the match. The then owner of the house, a Mr Grennan, had obligingly moved the radio set close to the open window so that the audience could hear the better. My, how times have changed, in these days of gadgets and cellular phones, modern day folk who speed by on the new Kilcarn Bridge, could scarcely comprehend such events, which occurred here by the roadside not all that long ago.

All the old maps show a large house on the site, including the big stables in the yard, so there was indeed a residence there at the end of the 18th century. At the top of Barry's Hill everything changes and we will have to depart from the thus far familiar route that can mostly be driven upon today. The section of road from here to Philpotstown Cross (Garlow Cross), wasn't cut and in use until after 1817 – from here to Dunshaughlin, in 1780, the turnpike still followed its original course along the banks of the River Boyne, through the Dowdstown estate and on across the Hill of Tara.

The old route of the road took us past a stone house on the right – this house was known to some as the Coachhouse and behind it there was a drinking well on the riverbank known as Saint Patrick's well. I have been told there once was a carving of the saint on a stone at the back of the well, but I have never seen it. At time of writing, the house is owned by Joseph Kinsella and has been in the possession of his family for some years – in earlier days, it was lived in by the Price family, who emigrated to England years ago. Though so far, I have been unable to discover any more of its history, the former name and its location on the edge of the road, would suggest that it had something to do with the operation of the road. Perhaps it may have been the location of the tollhouse for a time.

This stretch of the old road was known as Mill Lane, because it provided an entry to the old mill and several local houses. There was once a triangular shaped island of grass at the entrance to this lane beside its junction with the main road at the top of the little knoll known as Barry's Hill. Here, at the river side of the lane, stood a corrugated iron shed. For many years this was used by the County Council as a tool store – all through our youth we called it "the tin shed" and it was the source of many youthful tales – but when the new bridge was built, the shed was demolished as part of the realigning of the lane.

One of the aforementioned tales of the Mill Lane concerned the little grass triangle, the tin shed and a famous local drunk – the story was related to me by Jimmy Bradley (Young Jimmy, not Ould Jimmy) who later became my father in law. The time was in the early 1960s when Jimmy was in charge of the waterworks at the old mill. In the centre of the grass triangle was a big manhole, which gave access to a chart meter on the watermain about four feet underground. From time to time, when he was testing for water leaks, Jimmy had occasion to change the charts on the meter at regular intervals. On one such occasion, at midnight, Jimmy was down in the manhole, crouched down below ground level whilst changing the chart. He had a flashlight with him and was working away when he heard some loud singing as the drunk waltzed his pushbike up Barry's Hill and then a loud clatter as he threw the bike up against the old tin shed. Leaving the flashlight on the meter, Jimmy straightened up and popped his head up out of the manhole to see what was going on.

His rather abrupt appearance caused mayhem on that quiet summers night long ago. As Jimmy's head suddenly appeared, seemingly out of the ground, his face and grey hair illuminated by the flashlight down in the hole, the drunk, who was enjoying a pee up against the tin shed, let out a wail of terror and disappeared back down the hill from whence he had come; running on the winged feet of terror and travelling a lot faster without his old bike. Jimmy said that he could still hear him wailing all the way back across Kilcarn Bridge and on towards the town – like a demented Banshee he disappeared into the night, heading for the bright lights of Navan in the distance. His old bike remained there, lying against the tin shed for over a week – a silent testament to what wonderful energy sheer terror can infuse into ones legs. It can only be imagined the tales with which he regaled his drinking companions in the future – of how he had seen the fiery Devil himself rising up out of a hole in the ground at the Mill Lane at midnight.

The mill at Lower Kilcarn (the big mill) was formerly owned

by Mc'Canns of Drogheda and had several other owners over its chequered lifetime, originally it ground corn, then later was also used as a flax scutching mill. It operated until the latter part of the 19th century. Over the years, many tons of premium flour were ground on its millstones and hauled along the turnpike road to Dublin and elsewhere – no doubt contributing handsomely to the coffers of the road trustees in the process. I'm sure that the flax processed here, helped to produce many a fine garment to be worn by the ladies and gentlemen of the day. The site was taken over by Navan Town Council around 1900, the mill buildings being used to house machinery – the millers house was occupied by the waterworks superintendent for many years afterwards. When the town council took charge of the site, it was used as a waterworks, supplying the needs of the town of Navan for over one hundred years – indeed; the site is still in use as a waterworks at time of writing. In my father's youth, the old mill was famous for the great number of dances held in its old creaking lofts – he told me many stories of the escapades then and some yarns of events that happened during the Black and Tan era in the early 1920s. Old Jimmy Bradley (Ould Jimmy) ran the waterworks there from the early days around 1900 and only retired from active participation in its operation in the 1960s. He saw it progress from the days of water power, through steam, diesel and on to electrical power. A fine broad spectrum of experience to have on ones CV, and very unlikely to be repeated in the near future.

I must confess a personal interest in Kilcarn Mill, as I'm married to 'Ould Jimmy's' Granddaughter, whose father was the aforementioned 'young' Jimmy Bradley, the 'Devil' of the manhole and the drunk's worst nightmare. In my youth, I oftentimes swam at the skewed weir, indeed, my wife Marie taught me to swim there in exchange for driving lessons in my old Ford Anglia. In those days it was a beautiful place, almost idyllic, and many people, some local but others from Navan and elsewhere, came to swim in the reasonably clean river waters of the day. On the hot summer evenings, the grassy banks over by Boyne Hill and the stone 'river wall' on the Johnstown side might be thronged with both old and young prospective bathers – the laughter and merriment and the screaming of excited kids rang out on the summer air. But like everywhere else, modernity has caught up with this place also. Now the new sewerage works in the former Clooneen Wood disgorges into the river a short distance upstream at Dowdstown. So in the summer evenings the place is quiet now – except for the sullen roar of the Boyne waters as they tumble across the weir and the incessant drone of traffic on the nearby N3. In my memory I can still hear the merry laughter of the children of yesteryear, as they cavorted in the waters – and once more I wonder at the hidden price we pay for progress.

Going onwards towards Tara, the road passed the entrance to Lower Kilcarn, or Nether Kilcarn as it's named on the Taylor and Skinner map. Three of the old maps, the Longfield map, the OS of 1836 and Larkin's Map, all show a building at the intersection of the estate avenue and the turnpike road – I would assume that this was the gate lodge of the period. The present day house owned by Connie Farrell is built very close to the same spot, but it sits on the site of the actual old avenue. The gate lodge now standing at the N3 entrance to the estate, which is called Kilcarn Park, was built in

1888 and has an interesting inscription on a plaque over the door –
but more about this anon.

A couple of hundred yards or so further up the road, we
come upon the ruins of a very interesting building. In an earlier
chapter I call it a hostelry, but this is merely a flight of fancy of
mine, poetic licence so to speak – in fact I don't really know what
its use was, but I know that its remains still existed. In my youth, I
poked through its briar-covered ruins and wondered what the pile
of rubble was doing there in the middle of a field. At that time the
area was known as 'the little wood' and could be accessed through
an iron gate, which closes off the old route of the road, close by
Farrells house. Now, as I write, I have been told that these traces
have disappeared, both the ruins and the little wood being
bulldozed as part of land clearance. Some record of their existence
has been preserved however and can be discovered if you look
hard enough. They show up on the three aforementioned maps, in
fact on both the 1836 OS map and the Longfield map, and, are
shown in very good detail, especially when magnified. Two
buildings were on the site, to the right of the road, the side towards
the river, and they were laid out rather like the forecourt of a
modern day service station – with open access to the road and no
boundary walls in evidence. I haven't been able to discover any
more facts about this site, but in the absence of any contradictions,
I think it's reasonable to conclude that the place was some type of
hostelry, perhaps a roadside Inn or the tollhouse itself.

About a half mile further up the turnpike road, the entrance to
the estate at Upper Kilcarn is very interesting, as it was the centre
of a small network of lanes and avenues in times past. In my youth

and at time of writing, the estate was owned by the O' Kelly family and was (is) accessed by the 'new line' of the N3 main road to Dublin. In the past, it was owned by Major O' Kelly and at time of writing by Miss Pat' O' Kelly, his daughter – it's a well known stud farm and produced many noted racehorses over the years. In the 1780s, both it and Lower Kilcarn, were owned by Barry Esquire. The two estates have been in the possession of different occupiers in the intervening years. As mentioned, a laneway once led from the turnpike road up to the Rath on the Oldtown road at Pastor Hill, later, this was where the Parish Priest of Johnstown lived before moving down to the Parochial House behind Johnstown Church in the 1970s. Interestingly, Larkin's Map shows that there were once three Raths in close proximity to Pastor Hill, about 1812. This lane is shown on the Longfield estate map as being the property of Pastor Barry in 1819. The three maps all indicate an avenue connecting the Upper and Lower Kilcarn estates in those times, this avenue met the laneway very close to the present day N3 – the old line of the avenue can still be seen as I write. The Longfield map shows the lane running from Croboy Lodge (named Crohanboy on Larkin's Map – yellow hill?), and past old Kilcarn graveyard, once joined the Pastor Hill laneway about halfway between the turnpike and Oldtown. But strangely, Larkin's Map for some reason doesn't show either the Graveyard or the lanes.

Further on we come to the aforementioned mill at Upper Kilcarn (Little Kilcarn) and as stated previously, there was a mill on this site since around the late 1600s. Very little information is available about this mill, but the last known operator was named James Ledwich (sic), in 1860. Griffith's valuation of 1854 indicates that the house, corn-mill, offices, some land and a limekiln and quarry were leased from Charles Barry at an annual rateable valuation of £12 10s 0d. Local legend says that the miller's family were related to the famous later day poet Francis Ledwidge from Slane. I read that the millstones were moved down to Martry Mill, on the River Blackwater. (Ref' *the waters of the Boyne and the Blackwater'* by C. Ellison).

Recently I visited the old mill at Martry to check the veracity of this reference and met with the very affable proprietor of the establishment. James Tallon is the present day owner and the incumbent miller who runs the mill and produces 'stone ground' flour' for many customers. It was a fascinating experience to tour around such an old structure and see how things were done in olden times. To walk within the stone walls and beneath its low ceilings, to visualise the many centuries of absorbed wisdom and experience was indeed both a chastening and an uplifting journey in today's world of hustle and bustle. It was rather like a little trip on a time machine through times past, I saw many things enthralling to the engineering part of my psyche. Like the big gearwheels, some made of wood and others of cast iron, the old refractory bricks from the former kilns and the descriptions given by James of the methods used in their regular cleaning during his childhood. These were all glimpses of times that have almost gone forever. When I considered that the mills at Upper and Lower Kilcarn, contained systems such as those still in use at Martry, I once again marvelled at how cheaply we in Ireland have disposed of most of our ancient heritage.

What fascinated me most were the great millstones and the

beautiful symmetry and complexity of the mills operation, from the hopper to the flourbag. As my space is limited I cannot do justice to this ancient mill in these writings, but some day perhaps I may try.

I viewed the millstones belonging to the long disappeared mill at Upper Kilcarn, these were standing against the wall in the lower part of the mill – two very large French 'Burr Stones' in pristine condition. I also heard the story of their journey from Kilcarn and why they never ground even one grain of corn at Martry Mill. Seemingly, in the 1930s, with great effort and determination they were loaded onto horsedrawn drays, then transported down to their new home in Martry. On arrival, it was discovered that they wouldn't work at the new location on the River Blackwater, as their designed direction of rotation wasn't suitable. But all the effort was not in vain, their removal to Martry ensured their survival throughout the years of great change when many irreplaceable items were lost for posterity. As far as I know, the two old millstones are the only surviving mementoes of the mill at Upper Kilcarn, the only tangible proof that a mill ever existed there.

This tale of the millstones provides a clue to the precise location of the mill at Upper Kilcarn. Though the mills at the two locations were situated on rivers flowing in opposite directions, both were sited on the right hand bank of their respective rivers looking in the direction of water flow. As the fall in the rivers was much the same and Martry Mill has an undershot wheel, it is reasonable to conclude that the wheel at Upper Kilcarn was also of a similar design. The water head being insufficient to drive an overshot wheel, the direction of rotation would have been identical.

Hence the millstones should have been the same design for both mills, so, assuming the Kilcarn stones, now at Martry, were actually used to grind corn at Upper Kilcarn, why were they different? A closer examination of the OS map indicates that the Kilcarn Mill was sited on both the main riverbank and also on an island in the Boyne, with a building shown on each side of the millrace. The stones at Marty were probably from the mill sited on the island, therefore its wheel and millstones would have rotated in the anti-clockwise direction as opposed to clockwise if they had been located on the opposite side of the millrace.

Prior to the cutting of the 'new line' of the turnpike road, the present day N3, the only road access to the mill at Upper Kilcarn was via the old turnpike road – the latter day laneway from the N3 didn't exist then. In the 1880s, a family named Mongey, who I believe were related to the Ledwidge family, lived at the miller's old house and the laneway became known as Mongey's Lane – some of the older locals still call it by that name today. The men of the family were noted GAA footballers and three of them won medals with the Dowdstown team, which achieved victory in the Meath championship in 1887 and 1888. James Mongey was the Captain of that team, later beaten in the All Ireland series by Limerick Commercials, who went on to win the All Ireland championship.

In my youth, Kit Meehan and his wife Mary Jo' lived in the old house and we often visited there whilst walking in the Dowdstown woods and many other times in our pony and trap with our parents, who were great friends of the Meehans. Kit was a Ganger on the County Council and rode his bike around the local roads, supervising the workmen – he was a bit of a ventriloquist, he could throw his voice and often played havoc with us kids.

Few signs of the actual mill remained during our far off childhood; just some ruined stone buildings scattered along the riverbank. The weir and the millrace were still there, and the sound of the waters of the Boyne thundering through the gaps in the broken rampart was very frightening to our young senses. The weir ran askew across the river to the Ardsallagh banks on the other side – the millrace re-entered the main river some way downstream, almost opposite the residence at Upper Kilcarn, now O' Kelly's house. This formed a little knob of land in the Boyne known to us as the big island. The 1836 OS map shows two islands in the river downstream of the weir. Sadly, the islands, the weir and millrace are all gone – being demolished during the Boyne drainage scheme of the 1970s. I recall the cobblestone yard and the big orchard down towards the river – also, the many anecdotes we heard whilst drinking tea and eating bread and jam in the large flagstoned kitchen. We heard stories about the old mill and the Coachroad and how the place had been a sort of staging post or post-house, where the horses were changed on the big coaches that once ran by the front door. I know now these were merely yarns, but in those days we had no sense of time and to us then, it all seemed like it had happened just the day before – oh for those timeless happy days of our youth once more. Recently, a big modern house has been built on the site and most of the remaining traces of what had been there seem to have vanished from the landscape, yet another piece of our history is gone without a trace.

The junction with the old Drogheda road was about a quarter of a mile on past the old mill at Upper Kilcarn – just on the boundary of the townland of Dowdstown. On the way, in a small wood to the right of the roadside, there's a fine 'dug' drinking water well. It's about three feet in diameter and lined with masonry. The well was there in my youth and had a 'cowboy style' hand pump sitting atop it then. Though the pump is long gone, the well is still there at time of writing and blocked by a tree stump put there to stop animals falling in. This junction is shown on all three of the aforementioned maps – on the Taylor and Skinner map of 1778, it's clearly marked as the Drogheda Road. The Longfield map doesn't cover this particular section. Cross-referencing the maps indicates that the present day "Yellow Walls Lane", or Kilcarn Heights Road, as it's known to the swanks, was part of this road. The cutting of the new line from Philpotstown Cross (Garlow Cross) to Kilcarn isolated the short section running down through Major O' Kelly's field and it became obliterated and merged back into the landscape. I will cover this road in greater detail in a later book, titled *An ancient road in County Meath*. Larkin's Map and the 1836 map both show a little cluster of buildings, perhaps a small hamlet, on the Dowdstown side of the stream and close by the crossroads.

On past the junction, of which there is no trace nowadays, we come to the small stone bridge, which in our childhood we knew as Brian Boru's Bridge – some of the local historians, who know of its existence, call it Saint Patrick's Bridge, so take your pick. My father always called it by the former name and that's how I think of it today. It's a bridge that few people know about, as it's hidden in the woods and mostly covered by the luxuriant vegetation. The arched structure is very well built, about six feet high and about the same in river width – but its road width is remarkable, as it is over twenty feet or so, which indicates that it wasn't just any old bridge built for farm usage. Probably being built specifically, or widened, to carry the new turnpike road across the stream, about 1728 or thereabouts. Like so many such structures in Ireland today, it has fallen into decay due to lack of maintenance. Nature, and especially the ivy, is wreaking havoc with the ancient stonework and someday soon it will be just another pile of crumbling stones – perhaps to be used to stone face some modern dwellinghouse. The river that it spans is known to some as the Follistown River, a stream forming the boundary between the townland of Dowdstown and Kilcarn. Close by the bridge, on the River Boyne side of the road, there is an ancient Limekiln built into the high banks of the valley. I don't know its age, but it was very old when I was a child and playing hide and seek in the wooded area around it – perhaps it's older than the bridge itself and may have burned the limestone for the mortar used in its construction. Across the bridge and on the Dowdstown side of the stream, there's an old overgrown quarry – this was probably used for the stonework of the bridge and for many of the stone buildings on the Dowdstown estate, but we shall never know for sure. Once the bridge was crossed, the traveller was now on the lands of the Dowdstown estate.

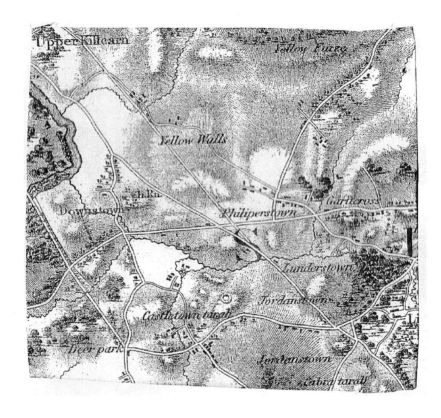

Section of Larkin's Map (1812 – 1817):

The turnpike road from Kilcarn to Jordanstown.

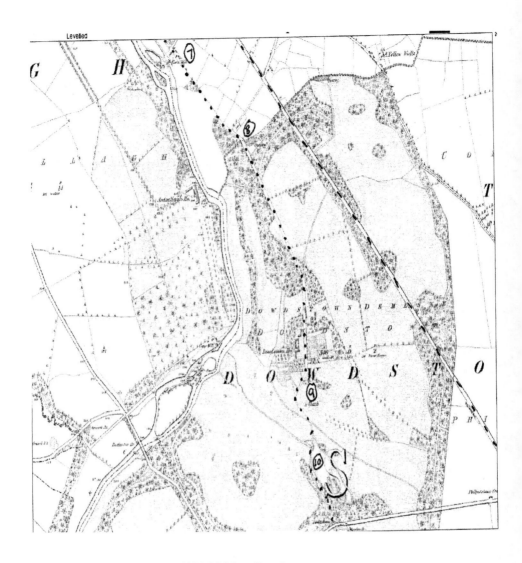

1836 OS Map: Dowdstown.

... denotes older line of road   – – – denotes newer line of road

7. Upper Kilcarn corn mill   8. Brian Boru's bridge

9. Walter Duff's church   10. Ornamental lake

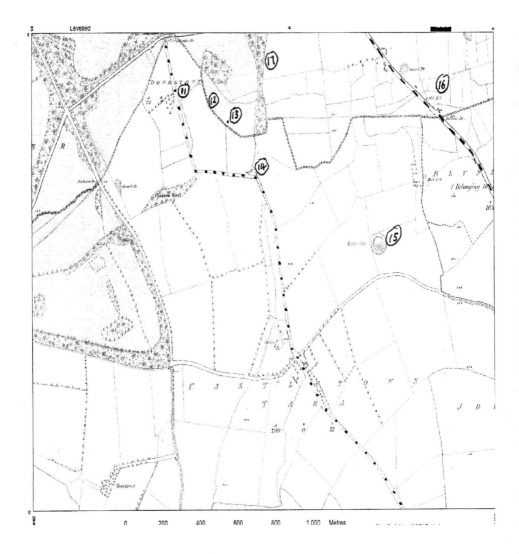

1836 OS Map: Castletown Tara.

… denotes older line of road   – – – denotes newer line of road

11. Herd's House (Griffith's valuation, 1854)   12. 'The Gabhra Island'

13. Site of mill shown on Larkin's Map   14. 'The Teacher's Cottage'

15. Rathmiles   16. Blundelstown Mill

17. 'The Sally Wood'

Chapter 4

Through Dowdstown to Churchill –
Hidden Secrets

Of all the sections of the old line of the turnpike road, which has virtually disappeared into the landscape, the part that ran through the Dowdstown estate is the most complex and difficult to disentangle and reconstruct into a form that makes sense. The reasons for this are many and include farming over the years, construction of the many avenues, the development of the Demesne, construction of artificial lakes and the diversion of the River Skane. This all happened within the boundaries of the estate itself, but the early part of the 19th century was to see massive redevelopment of the road network in the area. These changes included the cutting of the new lines of road from Dunshaughlin to Philpotstown Cross (Garlow Cross) and from there to Kilcarn Bridge, the building of Dowstown Bridge and Ambrose Bridge over the Skane and Bellinter Bridge over the River Boyne. All of these had a significant impact on the future of the old line of the turnpike road.

I have been unable to ascertain exactly when the Dowdstown estate came into the possession of the Taylor family.

The best available evidence would suggest that they gained ownership towards the end of the 18th century, perhaps in the 1770s, but this dearth of information is not overly important for the purpose of these writings. Normally, the Taylor and Skinner maps indicated ownership of the big estates through which the surveyed roads passed – usually depicting the big houses by small facsimiles and with the owner's name being clearly shown by text. In the case of the Dowdstown estate, this is not so – the presence of the house being indicated by a 'hollow square' depiction, with no indication of the owners name. I'm given to understand that this method was in common usage to represent large country houses whose owners were unidentified for whatever reason. Further research revealed that only the landowners financially supporting the survey venture in the 1770s, were rewarded by having their names included on the completed maps. There is evidence to suggest that the Taylors did not contribute financially to the survey. Local legend says that the Dowdalls of Athlumney owned Dowdstown prior to and during the rebellion of 1641 and the consequent Cromwellion Wars lasting into the 1650s. The Downs Survey of the 1640s and the Civil Survey of 1656 indicate that Lawrence Dowdall was the incumbent at the time of this particular conflict – the place being supposedly run by a steward who lived in the house. At the time, the estate was comprised of about 250 acres of land, a cottage style residence and the church. During the confiscations following the conflict, the Dowdalls were dispossessed and the land was given to a man named Robert Rochford. However, I have also heard that the Dowdalls regained possession with the restoration of the Monarchy, but were dispossessed once more following the Battle of the Boyne in 1690 and the subsequent Williamite confiscation's. If this were true, it would seem that they had the unhappy knack of supporting the wrong causes.

In olden times, from Brian Boru's Bridge, the road led towards the southeast, past the 21st milestone and headed in the direction of the stables and the rear of Dowdstown House. Nowadays, at time of writing, though the milestone is long gone from view, the path of the old road can be easily followed as it passed through the field and re-entered the wood at the fork in the avenues. It's used as a farm road now and has been for many years. During my early years, in the 1950s, Dad, my brother Tom and myself, often drove along this stretch on the pony and cart, hauling firewood from the Limekiln Wood and the Boyne Meadows. It was during these forays in the woods, in our never ending hunt for firewood, that I first heard about Brian Boru's Bridge and made the connection between this portion of the old road and the raised embankment running across 'the river field' behind our house.

As mentioned, about a quarter mile before we come to the probable location of the 21st milestone, a small laneway led off to the right and down towards the River Boyne – in former days we called it the Boyne Meadows lane. Passing between steep wild flower covered banks, it was then a cart track leading down into the swampy Boyne Meadows. The cutting for the laneway was obviously man made and the track ran down a steep incline to the meadows – there, it crossed a small stone Kesh spanning the Follistown River. Strangely enough, when this stream flowed under the old Coachroad at Brian Boru's Bridge, and entered the meadows, it swung sharply to the south, heading for a short distance in the opposite direction to the flow of the Boyne. Then it cut across the meadows and joined the big river above the shallows, or ford, at Ardsallagh House (once a castle) and just downstream of the long deep stretch known to us as 'the Boyne Deeps'. The stream formed the Mearing or boundary, between Dowdstown and Kilcarn parishes, therefore part of the Dowdstown estate was in Kilcarn parish and, significantly, the shallows, a possible ford, remained in Kilcarn. Because of this seemingly unnatural dogleg in the stream, it was intersected by the laneway, which crossed it by means of the aforementioned stone Kesh, or bridge. The laneway then headed across the Boyne Meadows towards the shallows in the Boyne. In our youth, in the summertime, I often walked down the old lane and crossed the Kesh, then sometimes removed my footwear and trodged across the Boyne, which had a shallow rocky bottom in that place. I visited Saint Brigid's well on the far bank, drank from the ancient fountain and admired the carving of the Saints head in the stonework, then returned across the shallow water. Supposedly, in much earlier times, in the sixth century AD, Saint Finian built the monastery of Escair-Branain (Ard-Bren-nDomhnach) somewhere on the Ardsallagh estate, but no trace of it has ever been found.

Though I have no proof of the matter, and, it's just my own pet theory, I would suggest that the original reason for the construction of the laneway and stone Kesh, was to provide the people in Ardsallagh with access to the Dublin road at suitable times of the year, when the Boyne was not in flood. At the time I'm referring to, Bellinter Bridge had not yet been built, nor had the road from Castletown to Cannistown; hence the residents of Ardsallagh had quite a long journey to go around by Kilcarn Bridge. Or perhaps the story has deeper roots in the past. The presence of Ardsallagh, with its reputed historical significance, on one side of the Boyne and what may have been one of the ancient *Slighte* on the opposite bank, would strongly suggest that the shallows here were indeed used as a ford at one time. The spelling of the name Ardsallagh is very important to its meaning – in his writings of 1836; John O' Donovan states that if the name was spelt Ard Salach it would mean 'the dirty height', others say it could be interpreted as 'the boggy height'. He also states that Ardsallagh means "the height of the Sallows, which word is possibly derived from an old English word, *Salh*, meaning a small Willow Tree – most historians seem to agree and conclude that it means 'the height of the Sallies'. If we pursue this logic, another slight spelling change, such as to Ath Sallagh, could alter its meaning to 'the ford of the Sallies'. I note with interest that the latest Discovery map of the area, at time of writing, indicates both of O' Donovan's spellings of the name – this would appear to apply the two meanings to the district. One version, presumably the English, is spelt Ardsallagh, whilst the other is spelt Ard Sallach. The wetlands in the area were renowned for their ability to sustain Willow Trees, during my youth, Sally trees grew profusely along the riverbank in the area of the shallows. Though many fords and shallows are mentioned as crossing places on the Boyne, I have never seen any reference to such a crossing between Ardsallagh and Dowdstown.

In the 1970s, the Boyne drainage scheme made drastic

changes to this area. Though the shallows have been blasted and dug, being considerably deepened and many tons of rock removed in the process, yet the Boyne is still relatively shallow in this place. The direction of the Follistown River has been altered and it now enters the Boyne on a straight course from Brian Boru's Bridge – but a tiny portion of the Dowdstown estate is still on its far bank, within Kilcarn. The stone Kesh is gone, either dug up or buried during the drainage scheme and no trace of it remains today. But the 1836 OS map clearly shows the dogleg in the stream and the little Kesh – so, even though I have a rather fertile imagination, I know that I'm not dreaming it up.

Over the years it would seem that the road took two slightly different routes from the Boyne Meadows lane to the rear of Dowdstown House. The Taylor and Skinner map of 1778 is the only map to show the milestones along the road, but because of the size and scale of this map it's impossible to determine their exact locations and most of them have disappeared over the years. During my childhood in the 1950s I recall seeing an ivy covered stone in the wood between Dowdstown House and 'the offices' building, as I walked along the cinder path to get a lift to school in Barney Allen's old Dodge Taxi. This stone was about three feet high, but though I was curious I never realised that it was a milestone from the old turnpike road. Recently, whilst talking to a friend about the old road he told me that he had seen the stone in the wood and there was some carving on its surface – the stone had been uncovered by some FAS workers whilst clearing pathways in the wood. If this was its original location it would seem that the former line of the road was very close to Dowdstown

House and about fifty yards to the west of its later route, as shown on the OS maps. Possibly the route of the turnpike was altered during the construction of the Demesne to align with the new stables?

The 1836 OS map shows the turnpike road passing on by the laneway, then gradually swinging towards the southwest to run on by the stables near Dowdstown house – nowadays these stone buildings are still there and are part of the farmyard. All the maps show the old turnpike road passing between the farm buildings and Dowdstown House. Initially, on the 1836 OS map, the single storey buildings along the road were shown, then on the 1882 OS map the two-storey present day "L" shaped building appears. The steward's house in the yard and the walled in garden can also be seen on the later maps, so the route of the road is quite clear, it followed the path of the present day farmyard avenue. But a short length of it is lost in the woods, close by the fork on the northern part of the avenue – the missing portion, about two hundred metres or so, can only be discerned from one of the maps mentioned. This particular section of the road is very clearly delineated on the 1836 OS map – it can be seen passing through the woods near where the avenue forks. This is very interesting, because it indicates that the woods, which were supposedly planted around 1816, were not planted over the turnpike road, as it must still have been in use at that time– this is a useful marker in tracking developments then.

I'm confident that I know the various routes the road took from Brian Boru's Bridge to the top of Dowdstown hill, near the old church. From here on, the route is very confusing and one could use the help of Sherlock Holmes to sort it all out. The turnpike road, now Dowdstown avenue, runs almost due west as it tops the hill, which overlooks the valleys of the Skane and the River Boyne. There's a beautiful view here, a vista of pastoral landscape and wooded river valley I have never seen surpassed – the Hill of Tara directly to the south frames the whole scene. This splendid view won't remain unspoiled for much longer, the broad swathe of the M3 motorway is being cut through the far side of the valley and is to cross the Boyne on an elevated bridge, just downstream of Bellinter Bridge and through the old beech wood at Oak Lodge.

At the top of the hill, the turnpike road swung to the left in a short curve and headed on a southerly course directly towards the Hill of Tara. About halfway down the slope and to the left of the road is the ancient graveyard and ruined building of Dowdstown Church. Not much remains today, just the remains of a square tower and a more modern wall surrounding the churchyard – with a couple of very ancient gnarled beech trees brooding over the scene. This was once a Cistercian Church belonging to Saint Marys of Dublin – being built by a Norman Knight named Sir Walter Duff, in the late1100s. Some people say the area derives its name from his surname and was originally called Duffstown, equally it could have been named after the Dowdalls, who owned it in times past. There are several more supposed derivations of the name, which I won't go into in these writings. The old building was once the church for the parish of Dowdstown, which was comprised of the townlands of Dowdstown and Philpotstown – these are no longer a parish but are part of the larger conjoined parishes of Johnstown and Walterstown. As a point of interest, the old townland of Dowdstown was actually in the parish of Tarah – it's shown thus on the 1836 OS map and is described as being part of that parish in O' Donovan's letters. It was very small, consisting of 22 acres, 2 roods and 3 perches, this townland formed the area known to us as 'the river field' during our younger days.

The whole district is steeped in hidden history. Recently, in 2005 and 2006, during archaeological digs in the area for the proposed route of the M3 motorway and some sewerage works, many artefacts were found and a local politician obtained the nickname of 'pots and pans' as a consequence. These finds included an ancient combined square and round Motte across the valley and behind Oak Lodge. I was variously informed that these remains dated back to about seven hundred years AD and one thousand years BC – take your choice. Closer to the old church, many smaller finds were made, including domestic utensils and human remains – leading some of the Archaeologists to surmise that the area around the church may have been used as a Cilleen. But, more pertinently from the point of view of the subject being discussed, namely ancient roads, the remains of several old roads were discovered in the immediate vicinity.

When I was a youngster, my father told me that there was once a crossroads on Dowdstown Hill (Church Hill), about halfway up and just below the wall of the churchyard. Here were two old iron gates, one on each side of the avenue – we called them "the cross gates", because of their location, and not because they were always angry – but perhaps in this name lies a clue to the history of the crossroads of former days. I'm not too sure where Dad found out about the ancient crossroads, he was always interested in such things – maybe he heard it from some of the old timers of his generation who were great at passing on such local history in the form of anecdotes? But wherever the information came from, research has shown that it was mostly accurate – this junction was the forerunner of the present day Philpotstown Cross (Garlow Cross), the meeting point of the ancient Dublin to Navan road and the Skryne road. The Taylor and Skinner map, the Longfield map and the 1836 OS maps show a road junction at this point in the old turnpike road. The first two maps indicate a fork in the road, whilst the OS map shows the remains of a road crossing the turnpike just below the old graveyard – I'll refer to Larkin's Map anon. Additionally, the Taylor and Skinner map indicates a 'T' junction between the two Skane crossings – this junction is hugely important in helping to unravel the mysteries of the ancient road system in Dowdstown. Dad maintained that the crossing road on Churchill was the old 'grand entrance' to Dowdstown House. This ran from the direction of the present day Philpotstown Cross, passing by the new 'priest's graveyard' up by the college wood. After crossing the turnpike/avenue at the 'cross gates', it ran along 'the well field', in a curve above the banks of the River Skane, and on by the haw-haw, through the daffodil beds and up towards the big house. I remember it very well. In those far off days the path of this old buried road was well defined, as it formed a cut out ledge along the hillside. This is one of the old roads unearthed in 'the well field' during one of the recent digs – it probably was the 'grand entrance' to the house in bygone days, providing a swanky access for visitors from the Dublin direction, driving along the then splendid valley of the Skane and allowing a magnificent view on the approach to the house. Whilst the more modest visitors used the tradesmen's entrance at the back, off the Coachroad by the farmyard.

I have no doubt that the other branch of this ancient crossroads was formed by the Dublin to Skryne road, which ran from Stoneybatter, through Ratoath. In those early days, Garlow Cross (Philpotstown Cross) didn't exist, as the new line of the Dublin to Navan turnpike road, the present day N3 from Dunshaughlin to Kilcarn hadn't yet been cut. The then line of the Skryne road was from Garlagh Cross (Old Garlow), past Jocks Cross, then, to the west of the present day location of Philpotstown Cross, it swung northwards. Skirting a big building, possibly a roadside Inn, it passed behind where Dan Norton's cottage stood in our youth and into Dowdstown, where it joined with the Dublin Navan turnpike at the old churchyard. As stated, there is much hidden history buried in the fields and woods around Dowdstown – the estate stands on the confluence of the Boyne and one of its larger tributaries, the Skane. The Motte unearthed during the dig on the M3 route, proves that it was a thriving area in ancient times, whilst the parish church would have been an additional hub of activity. During the dig at the ancient Motte, I saw the remains of an old stone paved road, or pathway, that headed westwards towards Bellinter and eastwards towards Walter Duff's old churchyard across the Skane – it was very narrow, perhaps five feet or so in width, but clearly defined and well paved. Who knows whence it came from or to where it once led? These and possibly many other factors of which we are unaware, together with Kilcarn

Bridge being the only dry crossing of the Boyne in the area, makes the notion of the junction here of two main roads from Dublin a perfectly sensible proposition.

The mention of olden times and strange occurrences, the site of the old crossroads on Churchill, just below the ancient churchyard, was the scene of a very strange happening, which we witnessed in our far off childhood.

One day, sometime around 1952, whilst we were messing around in the river field, on our way back from Tara, we had a very weird experience, which we later called the 'disappearing army'. Both my brother Tom and myself recall this event very well – some other neighbourhood kids were with us at the time, altogether there was a group of about six or seven of us playing in the field. We were over near the bend on the Gabhra; suddenly we all heard a sound like the beating of a drum. We looked all around but could see nothing to account for this strange sound. The noise continued, so we searched further afield. We looked across the road, over towards Dowdstown Hill, or Churchill, as we called the place – we had a clear line of vision in those days, as the swamp wood had been bulldozed, then we saw a very strange sight. Coming down the avenue and skirting Sir Walter Duff's ruined church, was a body of marching men. They all seemed to be clad in dark uniforms and were heading towards us. At the same time we noticed two figures, clad in bright red, running away from the old church, down 'the well field' towards the river Skane and in the direction of the recently discovered Motte. We didn't know what the hell was going on but we got very excited and decided to go and have a look. We ran like mad, out of the field and across

Dowdstown Bridge, then up the avenue. Much to our surprise and consternation, when we rounded the pumphouse (the ram) and looked up Church Hill, there was nothing there. All the activity we had seen a few minutes earlier had ceased, not a human being – or a ghost – was in sight. It was absolutely amazing, so much so that I can still feel the sense of wonder as I write these words.

We searched the avenues; up by Dowdstown House and back around by the college but saw nothing to explain the mystery. We weren't drinking or we hadn't had any magic mushrooms on Tara, so where had everyone gone? Also there was no sign of the two 'redcoats' we had seen running down towards the Skane. To this day it remains a mystery, when we told our parents they just laughed at us. But we talked it over amongst ourselves, when we got together, and it remained a lively subject of debate for many a long day.

Gradually it faded away over the intervening years, but it still remains clear in my mind's eye when I dredge it up. In fact, a few weeks ago, when I was musing over old memories with my brother Tom, he brought up the subject and he remembers it well, so it wasn't just my imagination. Whether it was human or ghostly, I shall never know but local legends were common enough about the old church.

One of the legends was that Oliver Cromwell burned down the church on his way to attack Trim, following the massacre at Drogheda; I'm sure that some of his men were dressed in red clothing! Mind you, the said Mr Cromwell got blamed for most things in those times, some of which never even happened.

Recently, during an Archaeological dig around the church,

many human remains and other artefacts were found. Indeed, so many items were uncovered the proposed development was changed, as it would have been prohibitively expensive to complete a proper dig in the area. It is possible that this area may have been a "Killeen" (Cilleen), a burial place for un-baptised children and adult sinners, such as executed felons. Whether or not this particular childhood experience was physical or spiritual, I shall never know. To a certain extent the recent discoveries explain the creepy feelings, which I often experienced whilst walking or cycling down Dowdstown avenue late at night

Larkin's Map paints a slightly different picture than the OS maps, but it confirms that the Skryne road did indeed join the Dublin Navan Turnpike road somewhere in Dowdstown. Peter O Keefe maintains that, though most of Larkin's Map was drawn around about 1812, that the map wasn't actually printed until 1817, when the new line of the turnpike road, from the newly formed Garlow/Philpotstown Cross to Kilcarn Bridge, was already cut and in use. The map shows both configurations, the old and the new, of the roads around Garlow Cross at that period and hence it's very revealing and provides a great insight into the redevelopment of the road networks in County Meath then. Larkin indicates that at the time, the Skryne road joined the turnpike to the north of the old church and not to the south as shown on the other maps. This junction could be at the fork in the avenue, on the Navan side of the farmyard and there's some evidence to show this might indeed be the case. This doesn't necessarily contradict the other maps, as they were all surveyed at different periods. It's possible that the difference could be accounted for by road realignments during the years, as the 1836 OS map shows only the remains of the road passing through Dowdstown, which was obviously disused by then. As mentioned, there were a great deal of changes taking place in the local road networks at that time – I'll cover this particular seeming anomaly in a later chapter.

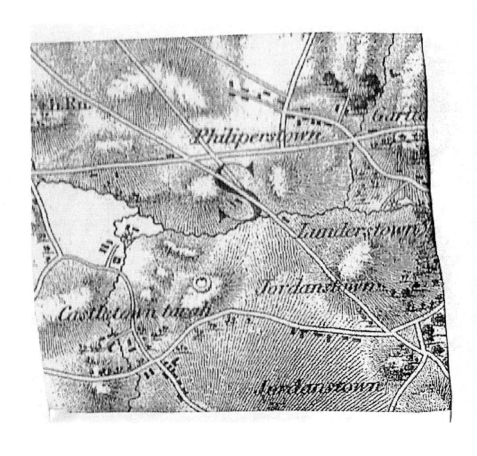

Section of Larkin's Map (1812 – 1817):

The turnpike road through Philpotstown Crossroads, showing the three different lines of the road.

Chapter 5

From Walter Duff's Church to Clooneen

There's a belief held by some that there was once a castle in the present day townland of Dowdstown. There are many ruined castles in the area, which are well known, such as Riverstown Castle, the ruins of the castle in Castletown Tara and the old ruined castles at Walterstown (Monkstown) and Asigh (Assey), Balsoon, Trubley, Craystown and Scurlockstown. Though some of these have almost entirely disappeared, yet they are well recorded. There was also a castle across the Boyne in Ardsallagh at one time, as well as the castles in Athlumney and Skryne – so the area was pretty well endowed by castles and towerhouses. But where was the supposed castle in Dowdstown? I was born and reared on the Dowdstown estate, and as a child I played in every nook and cranny – consequently, I practically knew every blade of grass and clump of bushes in the area. I never found the ruins of any castle, nor even a pile of stones that might indicate its presence. The earliest surveys, the Downs survey of the 1640s and the Civil survey a decade later, both refer to a "cottage style residence" on the estate, there is no mention of a castle. So, at least from around the middle of the 17th century, there appears to be no solid evidence that there was ever a castle on the estate or the townland as we know it today. A clue to the missing castle can be found in the oft' mentioned Taylor and Skinner maps. One prominent historian supposes that a castle once existed in Dowdstown mainly because one such ruined castle is shown on this map of the area, which was surveyed in the 1770s. In my opinion, these are the ruins of the old church, as so depicted on all the other maps – perhaps the surveyors mistook these ruins, dating from the late 12th century, for a castle. There is another possibility, which I think is highly unlikely, that either Dowdstown House or the ancient church was built on the site of an existing castle – but we shall never know for sure.

Further research provided another possible solution to this riddle from the past and indicates how some items of local knowledge can persist through the generations. I recently carried out a further perusal of the Civil survey of Dowdstown (1656), but found no reference to a castle under this heading. Then in the section on Philpotstown I found what I was looking for – a clear reference to a Castle and a thatched house in that townland. This appears to indicate there was a castle in the ancient parish of Dowdstown, but it was located in the townland of Philpotstown. As my space is limited, I will cover this subject in greater detail in my other book "*An ancient road in County Meath*".

However, enough about castles, back to the turnpike road and its tortuous passage through Dowdstown. Earlier I mentioned an old road that once skirted the swampy valley of the River Skane in Dowdstown. This road actually existed and was not another product of my imagination. When I first studied the 1836 OS map of the area, I was immediately struck by the big letter "S", the first letter of the name Skreen, which sat astride this particular part of the map. I was annoyed because it seemed to totally obscure the area including the ornamental lake, which was once in this spot. Then I noticed that the "S" provided some clues in itself – a wavy line that I thought was a fault in the old map, turned out to be the line of a road or path. Closer examination indicated it was in fact a road, as the drafters of the map had cut it through the "S" and it stood out boldly. This was the clue required and helped solve one of the problems of the passage of the old road through Dowdstown, which had been bothering me for some time.

I had always wondered why, if given the choice, a road builder would bridge a larger river twice, instead of bridging a much smaller river just once. This is what seemed to have happened to the turnpike road on its passage across the Skane at Dowdstown. The road crossed the river near the present day Dowdstown Bridge and again, a short distance downstream, crossed the larger sized river, which had been engorged by the addition of the waters of the Gabhra. I was puzzled as to why the builders hadn't diverted the road slightly to the east and bridged the much smaller Gabhra just once, then continued the road up the lesser gradient on that side and on up the hill by the old church. The line through the big "S" on the map shows that this was in fact the course of the road at one time – possibly before it was changed to a turnpike in the early part of the 1730s. Probably once being the path of the more ancient road running from Tara towards Navan and beyond. The northern end of this small section of older road was discovered recently in one of the aforementioned archaeological digs and caused much head scratching amongst the learned experts. It was a well built stone and gravel roadway about twenty feet wide and was on the exact location and orientated in the same direction as shown by the big "S" on the 1836 OS map. To the south, and on the same map, directly in line with this old section of road, there's a wooden bridge shown crossing the River Gabhra. This would seem to me to be the final confirmation that the ancient road from Tara, pre 1730, once skirted to the east of the swampy valley of the Skane at Dowdstown.

The route of the turnpike followed the present day line of Dowdstown Avenue, from the churchyard to the lodge gates on the present day Trim road. You might well ask how I know this and how I could state it so positively? My answer is, "because of a bridge that no longer exists".

To explain this seeming conundrum, it's necessary to revisit my childhood memories once more. The year is about 1952 and my brother Tom and myself oftentimes stood on the stone arched bridge carrying the avenue across the River Skane in Dowdstown. This bridge has no stone breast-wall on either side, but is protected by ornamental iron handrails and we knew it then as the swimming pool bridge, because there was an outdoor swimming pool in that spot long ago. This pool was built sometime in the 1940s to provide swimming facilities for the students in Dalgan Park Seminary. The pool was to the left of the avenue as you looked up towards the old churchyard on the hill, and the Skane flowed over a mossy lichen covered waterfall, or weir, into the pool, then onwards to the Boyne. Three boyscouts were drowned in the pool, at the waterfall, a few years earlier, in 1948 – this had cast a very dark shadow over our young lives and we dreaded the spot for many years thereafter. But our main interest at the time wasn't in the soft murmuring of the Skane tumbling over the waterfall or the beautiful pastoral setting – no, we were very interested in the big gangs of workmen digging out a diversion to the river close by. Two gangs of men, one on each side of the avenue, were hand digging a new course for the river, to take it under the other stone bridge located further back along the avenue towards the lodge at the Trim road.

We watched with great interest as the workmen dug out the oozy muddy path of the new riverbed, from the serpentine bends of the old river course that once took the full flow of the Skane under the bridge and across the weir by the pool. This new course took it on a different route and under the old stone arched bridge, before it rejoined the path of the Skane, just downstream of the swimming pool. A small side stream remained on the old riverbed to keep the pool supplied with fresh water. We both recall the bridge very well, mainly because we witnessed the diversion of the river back then, but this stone bridge is no longer there. Most of it was swept away by the great flood of the 8th of December 1954 – and we saw the remaining part of the broken arch immediately after the rest of the bridge had been wrecked by the flood. The whole downstream side of the section, about three metres in width, had been carried away by the raging floodwaters. At the time we wondered why the remaining stonework was so regular, with no jagged edges. At the time, a couple of spruce tree trunks were placed across the yawning chasm, these, together with the few feet of the stone arch, became the avenue bridge for over a year or more. We often drove the pony and cart over this makeshift crossing – I remember it very well indeed. A short time later, if I recall correctly it was1956, the remains of the stone bridge were dug out and a concrete bridge built in its place. This is the bridge that carries the Dowdstown Avenue across the Skane at time of writing – the river has remained on its present course since those days.

To understand the significance of the previously described events of our early years, it's necessary to return to the 1730s, when the old road was upgraded to a turnpike road – in my opinion, this is the likely scenario then. There is much evidence to suggest that in the late 1770s, todays road from Bective and Trim was routed more or less on its modern line until it came to what nowadays is known as Bellinter Crossroads – but where did it go after that? The aforementioned Bellinter Crossroads, Dowdstown Bridge, Garlow Cross (Philpotstown Cross) and the present day linking roads hadn't yet been built – I would contend that the road from Bective once ran across the old stone bridge in Dowdstown, destroyed many years later in the 1954 floods. The route from Bellinter Cross would have been on the higher ground above the swamp, then it swung to the left (northeast), crossing the stone bridge and joining the old line of the Dublin road near its junction with the Skryne road, close by the churchyard. People ploughing the nearby fields have told me that from time to time they have dug up parts of an old stone road in this area and they wondered about it. The line of this buried road ran roughly from the Bective/Trim road towards the avenue bridge over the Skane. If this theory is correct, the old stone bridge in Dowdstown must have been very old, probably predating 1730 – but like many other things in the area, we shall never know for sure.

When it was decided to change the status of the Dublin to Navan road to a turnpike, or tollroad, part of the upgrading involved rerouting the old road – from the junction at the Clooneen Wood, straight across the flood plain of the River Skane to the Skryne road at the crossroads by the churchyard on the hill. This effectively removed the section crossing the wooden bridge on the Gabhra and running to the east of the swamp. The new route took the road across the newly built causeway, or embankment, and to the banks of the Skane, close by where Dowdstown Bridge was later built to carry the Bective/Trim road across the combined rivers of the Gabhra and Skane, then up to Philpotstown Cross (Garlow Cross). This alteration of the route involved the building of only one new bridge across the river, and the widening of the existing stone bridge carrying the Bective/Trim road over the rivers, as described. With the alteration to the route, the Bective/Trim road now joined the turnpike at a fork, to the south of the old stone bridge. During our youth, the remains of this forked junction were still visible in 'the gravel pit wood' beside the bridge, but we never knew its significance then. This is the junction, which I referred to earlier as being shown on the Taylor and Skinner map as a 'T' junction. Just like at Kilcarn Bridge, there's strong evidence to suggest that an existing bridge was widened to accommodate the bigger coaches on a turnpike road. The manner of its destruction in 1954 would tend to support this contention. With the older wider downstream portion being carried away, leaving a clean profile on the surviving upstream section – on its own, this narrow portion of the old bridge could scarcely have been wide enough to provide more than a footbridge. When the new stretch of road was built, it crossed the Skane at its confluence with the Gabhra, then ran along the present day route of the avenue and recrossed the river at the previously described widened stone bridge. From the stone bridge, there most likely was a small causeway built as far as the road junction below the churchyard. This is the way I visualise the route of the road at the start of its turnpike era in the early 1730s, or very shortly thereafter.

Then, about 1814 –1816 everything changed again, with the development of the Dowdstown Demesne. An artificial lake was formed upstream of the stone bridge and the course of the river was altered. The bridge and weir, which we later knew as the swimming pool bridge, was constructed and the weir became an ornamental outflow into the re-routed river. A dam or high causeway was built across the swamp, from the widened stone bridge to the bottom of the hill by the churchyard. At the northern end of the dam a sluiceway was constructed to control the level of the lake and I suspect it was used as a water conduit for operating a hydraulic ram, or hydrostat. This would have been used to pump water up to the house. The reason why I make this assumption is, that in later years, in our childhood, the area was always known as "the ram" – though I'm not sure when the ram was installed, I'm certain that there was one there at some time, as they were a very common feature in the big estates in those times. All these features can be seen in detail on the 1836 OS map, the lake, the weir and sluice conduit, together with the new bridge, are plain to see, (the remains of the sluice winch, the sluice and stone built conduit being still there as I write). The old stone bridge is not shown on the maps, so I assume that it was blocked off to maintain the water level in the lake. This still leaves at least one question unanswered – if the River Skane was as good a salmon river then, as it later became, how did the salmon surmount the weir to get upriver to their spawning grounds at its headwaters?

This is the best explanation that I can give as to why two stone arched bridges were built within fifty yards of each other – to carry a dead straight section of roadway across an equally straight section of river. And why the river now flows under a concrete bridge and the remaining stone bridge lies idle, with only a dry floor beneath its fine stone arch and not a trace remaining of either the weir or the swimming pool.

I'm as certain as anyone can ever be, that the present day route of Dowdstown Avenue, from the churchyard to the lodge on the Bective/Trim Road, is the line of the turnpike road – from about 1730 until the demise of the road. Now we come to the vexed question of the first bridge across the Skane, at the Gabhra confluence near Dowdstown Bridge and the missing causeway I remember once formed an embankment across the river field and towards the Clooneen Wood to the south. At the time of writing, where once the turnpike road crossed the Skane at Dowstown Bridge, there is now a stone semicircle built into the western side of the extended breast wall of the bridge. People wonder why this was built, but the explanation is simple – it was there to provide a turning arc, which enabled the large horsedrawn coaches to sweep around and up the avenue. May Lynch, who lived in the lodge across the road, for many years used the space as a little garden and kept a wonderful array of flowers growing there providing a colourful display for the travellers on the road in times past.

All the maps previously mentioned, show that the turnpike road crossed the Skane immediately to the west of its confluence with the Gabhra. The crossing must have been a bridge, as the road builders had gone to a great deal of trouble and expense in building the causeway in order to raise the road clear of potential floods – hence, fording the river makes no sense. Though in my youth, I have seen much excavating done along the riverbank, yet I have never seen any sign of bridge abutments, or even a few stones, which might suggest the presence of a bridge in this spot. My brother Tom has some memories, which might supply a clue to the missing bridge. He says that he remembers a gang of workmen hand digging and realigning the river at its approach to the bridge. He thinks the river once curled to the south for a short distance, before turning back and flowing under Dowdstown Bridge on a straighter line. This was a common enough feature at small older river crossings, and was a method used to protect some stone bridges from damage being caused by the angular impact of floodwaters. If this memory is accurate, it's possible that the remains of the bridge abutments lie buried at the bottom of the river field, about where the old causeway ended close by the riverbank.

Alternatively, it's possible that this crossing of the river could have been by a wooden bridge. The Longfield estate map, whilst not very clear, provides some insight into the matter – it appears to show walls on each side of the turnpike road at the river crossing and distinctly shows a crossroads. This would tend to support the idea that it was a stone bridge and further suggest that both the turnpike road and the new line of the Trim to Drogheda road were in use concurrently, around 1822. The causeway, or embankment, disappeared sometime after 1971, that's the last time I can recall seeing it. I drove a tractor along it in that year, whilst drawing firewood during the cutting down of the trees in the clump wood.

Crossing the bridge, whatever its construction, we proceed along the causeway, or embankment and come to what I have previously referred to as a hostelry – this is an intriguing part of the road for me in particular. In my childhood there was a wood here, which we referred to as 'the clump' or 'the round wood'. It was a small copse, with no undergrowth, and contained a mixture of oak, beech, elm, chestnut and lime trees – I recall the chestnuts very well, as we often obtained our "conkers" here. On the northeastern boundary of the wood lay an old ruin, which in those days was completely overgrown by nettles and briars, but we never knew what was there beneath all the tangle of greenery. This was the remains of what I described earlier as the hostelry in Dowdstown.

The route of the M3 motorway is across this spot and the old ruins will be completely covered by the new super highway, also a tollroad. Additionally, the Trim Drogheda road is to be re-routed once again and will cross the M3 close to this spot, so the beautiful view of the Hill of Tara, so often admired from Dowdstown Bridge, will be blotted out by concrete bridges and high earthen embankments. The road from Bellinter Cross to Garlow Cross, built around 1814 and which holds so many fond memories for me, will be but a cul-de-sac at both ends.

As well as a huge sadness, there's also a touch of irony in

this for me, as almost two hundred and eighty years after the original tollroad was built through the valley, now another tolled road is about to be built over it in this place. The crossing point is only about a couple of hundred yards from the house in which I was born and where I spent my youth. Its path will cross the River Skane in the exact spot where we built our dams across the Skane, to deepen the river so that we could paddle in its clear sparkling waters. But unlike the old tollroad, which has merged back into the surroundings and barely left a trace of its former presence – I doubt that the same will happen to its usurper. Even when it too falls into disuse, as it ultimately will, the scars on the landscape will remain forever – a monument to what? The beautiful valley will never be the same again.

At least one good thing resulted from the proposed construction of the new highway through this place – the old ruin was excavated and I discovered what had been lurking under all the briars and nettles, where oftentimes I had been scratched and stung during my far off youth. It was the ruins of a fine stone built residence and outbuildings, which had one very unusual feature for its time – the floor was constructed from red "fired bricks". This building is located very close to the route of the turnpike road, about twenty feet or so to the west of the roads edge – near the spot where the causeway ended and the road resumed its slightly raised path across the fields towards the Clooneen. The excavations also uncovered parts of the old gravel roadbed, so it was not a cobbled road – the standard turnpike roads of that era were topped with gravel. The Archaeologists on the dig didn't seem to be aware of the causeway that once carried the turnpike across the river bottoms, and that parts of the old excavated road would have been several feet below the tollroad that ran atop the causeway. This is quite interesting, as it appears to suggest that the new line of the road had first been constructed at the original ground level with the causeway being built later – probably in response to flooding of the highway. But now we shall never know, as it's not likely that anyone will dig up the new motorway to discover the answers from the past.

The building in question shows up on the 1836 OS maps and the later OS maps of 1882 and 1911. It's also clearly shown on Larkin's Map and the Longfield estate map of Dowdstown – but very little other information is available. The Longfield map, though the copy I obtained from the National Library is barely legible, does provide some additional information and is very useful if interpreted in conjunction with the other maps. It shows the turnpike road running across the field from Dowdstown Bridge, but it ends at the edge of the estate, over by the Clooneen – though significantly, it clearly names it as the "old road to Dublin". The particular map must have been drafted after 1817, and prior to its date of 1822, as it indicates the new line of the Dublin road from Garlow Cross to Kilcarn, which wasn't cut until then. It also shows the various plots of land leased to different tenants around or before 1822. This indicates that the Dowdstown estate was obviously not used as a residential farm by its then owners, but was leased out as a series of smallholdings. The building along the road was part of one such holding at the period mentioned, being marked as number 19 and appears to be leased to someone named Mahon at the time. Though I researched Griffith's valuation records of Dowdstown parish for the year 1854 and couldn't find any reference to anyone of that name – none of the records seem to go back as far as the era of the turnpike road in its heyday.

I'm convinced that this house and outbuildings were built as part of the original upgrading of the turnpike road – the archaeologists who performed the dig have dated it as early 18th century. This would tend to support the notion that its purpose had something to do with the operation of the road. It's also reasonable to suggest that because of the steep gradient up the Hill of Tara, starting nearby, that this may well have been a staging post, (Post House – ref' section on Blackbull)) where the horses were changed for the heavy pull ahead. It certainly wasn't any ordinary humble dwelling, as it was too well constructed and had a very unusual brick floor. Also, it was built on part of the Dowdstown estate, so it wasn't the dwelling place of a substantial farmer or a tenant of a large holding. Therefore, if it wasn't part of the road operations, what other purpose could it have served? At the time, the estate was typical of one owned by a mostly absentee landlord and run by an agent – there being very few dwellings and the gate lodges weren't built until around the 1890s. So what was the purpose of the substantial stone dwellinghouse and outbuildings standing in the middle of 'the river field' in Dowdstown in the 1780s?

From the mysterious building in 'the river field', the turnpike continued on towards Tara. At the south end of the field was the Mearing drain between the townland of Dowdstown and the townland of Castletown Tara – crossing this boundary, a wet ditch, we come to the Clooneen Junction, a few yards into the townland.

On a point of interest – previously I referred to the fact that Dowdstown was a parish consisting of the townlands of Dowdstown and Philpotstown. Referring to the OS map of 1836, it would seem that there were once two Dowdstown townlands. One being in the parish of Dowdstown and the smaller one in the parish of Tara. This small townland seems to have been part of the townland of Castletown Tara, located in the parish of Tara and possibly a detached portion of Dowdstown parish. The smaller townland was to the south of the Rivers Skane and Gabhra and consisted of the area I refer to as the 'river field', which was an irregular shaped field of 22 acres 2 roods and 3 perches. O' Donovan's letters refer to this townland under the heading of the parish of Tara and the area is clearly marked as a separate entity on the 1836 OS map, but not on the later series of OS maps. When I discovered this 'new townland', I re-examined Griffith's valuation and found a reference to this portion of land and what I would assume to be the mysterious house alongside the old road. In the section under the parish of Tara I found that in 1854, the field was leased by Col. Thomas E. Taylor to a James Topham. This man seemed to have most of the Dowdstown estate on lease at the time. The house was listed as a 'herds house and offices' with a rateable valuation for the whole property of £16 5s 0d. This is a little curiosity I came across during research, which I thought to mention and it helped to solve another little problem further along the road.

Section of Larkin's Map (1812 – 1817):

Showing Garlagh Cross, Tara, Lismullen, and Skryne.

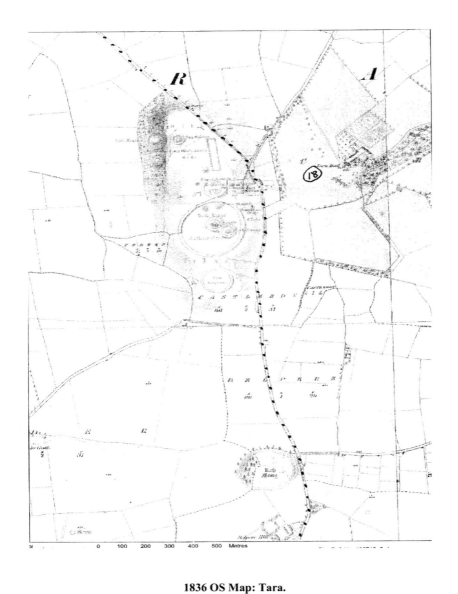

1836 OS Map: Tara.

...   denotes older line of road   − − −   denotes newer line of road

18. Tara Hall (Newhall)

Chapter 6

From the Clooneen Across Tara to Ballyna Cross

As children we walked the path of the old tollroad, crossing 'the river field' on the remains of the causeway and climbing the fence beside the wet ditch and into Barney Norton's field, this took us into the townland of Castletown Tara. We were on one of our many trips to the famous hill, to play our childish games and keep ourselves amused in those far off days when the sun always seemed to be shining. We had been told that our path had once been the old road to Dublin, but we weren't very interested in such things then, our main concern was about Barneys big bull, the fearsome creature about which we had been told so many stories. When we climbed into the new townland, we cared not a whit for such things as townlands and tollroads. Being more concerned about making it safely to the big iron gate at the bottom of the Tara lane and climbing it rapidly to the safety of the quiet and secluded laneway on its other side. Though we didn't know it then, this was once a crossroads on the old turnpike road, the place I now refer to as the Clooneen Junction.

The road intersection is shown on the Taylor and Skinner map and Larkin's Map, but not on the 1836 OS map – the reason for its omission from the latter map is because the other leg of the road had become disused and had probably merged with the surrounding landscape once more. I had always been puzzled as to why the turnpike ran straight across the fields from Dowdstown bridge, then made a sudden ninety degrees turn to the east at the Clooneen Wood. When I discovered Larkin's Map in Navan Library a few years ago, much lost information was revealed and many things puzzling me were resolved.

William Larkin was an engineer and surveyor who was heavily involved in the design and construction of many of the road realignments in County Meath in the late 18th and early 19th centuries. His famous maps of the County are very revealing and oftentimes provide the final pieces of many of the jigsaw puzzles posed by the former paths of some of the ancient roads in this area. Though the maps are of a very small scale and are consequently quite difficult to follow, they can be very effective when scanned onto a computer and magnified – then cross-referenced with the OS maps of a slightly later period. I have great faith in them, as they have helped me enormously in solving many riddles – some of the discoveries I made from studying these maps have astounded me. If anyone knew the area well during this period of great change, it was William Larkin, as he was involved in designing many of the road alterations.

When the map showed the old road from Dowdstown to Tara, veering to the right and on through where the Clooneen Wood once grew, I was both astonished and delighted. This explained the reason for the sudden 90 degrees bend in the turnpike road, which had been puzzling me ever since those childhood walks. As it transpired, it wasn't a right-angled bend, it was in fact a fork in the road, which I now call the Clooneen Junction. The left branch was the continuation of the turnpike road across Tara, the right branch being the road onwards towards Kilmessan.

Armed with this knowledge, I re-appraised the Taylor and Skinner map and found the junction on it also, with the Kilmessan road truncated and not marked as such. Later, I poked around in the small remaining section of the Clooneen Wood and found the path of the old road to Kilmessan, exactly where it was shown on Larkins Map. It could be followed where it angled up the steep ridge and disappeared at Swanton's field ditch.

If we follow the left fork, the turnpike enters the stretch known to us as the Tara lane. Nowadays, a short section of this old lane is almost overgrown and is but a muddy entry to a field at the back of the sewerage plant, the unlovely usurper of the beautiful Clooneen Wood. Typically of modern Ireland, it looks likely that this section of the ancient roadway is to be "absorbed" and swallowed up by the garden of a new house under construction at time of writing. Yet one more memento of our ancient heritage, the survivor of wars and famines down through the years, will be removed from the landscape by progressive Ireland. In our far off youth it was an almost enchanted place, as I described previously. Here Larkins Map provides yet another surprise – it shows that at one time in the past there was a water driven mill close by the turnpike, on the River Gabhra, which flowed nearby. Access to the mill and several buildings being provided by a laneway leading from the turnpike road beside the Kesh carrying the road across the small stream. The little stream joining the Gabhra here and which I described in an earlier chapter, rises over in Cardiffstown, at the bottom of the western slopes of Tara – flowing on through Castletown and passing close by the ruins of the castle and under the turnpike before joining the Gabhra. I had always wondered why the river was routed in such a way – it flowed from the east, through Lismullin and Dillon's Bridge, then splits in two as it came to the Mearing, where once the tall oaks of the Sally Wood dominated this corner of Dowdstown. A short distance further on, within the Dowdstown estate, both parts of the river rejoin. The field between the two branches of the stream was known to us then as the Gabhra Island – on the eastern end of which once grew the southern section of the aforementioned Sally Wood. The reason for the split in the river had always eluded me and it didn't seem to make any sense – but the mill shown on Larkin's Map, at the junction of the Cardiffstown stream, solved the riddle for me. This stream was the last one to pay tribute to the Gabhra, hence a mill at this place would obtain the maximum volume of water at any point on its course before joining the River Skane. The reason for the long diversion was to provide a head and tailrace for the watermill, which in turn caused a differential head across the millwheel. The split course of the river shows up on all the OS maps and on Larkins Map, but not on the Taylor and Skinner map, as this only indicates the main roads and some of the big houses. The Longfield map isn't clear enough to make out any details in the area.

Larkin marked many of the small local mills on his maps. These included the mill on the Skane in Kilmessan (Arnold's Mill),

Lismullin Mill, also known as "the Kings Mill" and on the Gabhra less than a mile upstream – three mills on the Nanny, including MacNamara's Corn Mill near Fairlands Cross, the mill near Kenstown, which in our youth was Daly's sawmill, and the water mill near Balrath. He also shows the old windmill at Balrath, the two mills at Clavinstown and the mill on the Herley River (Hurley or Caman, as Gaelige) near Rathfeigh, but strangely enough, he doesn't show any of the mills on the Boyne, except possibly Bective Mill. All the water mills are depicted by a small facsimile of a waterwheel, a tiny circle with seven spokes radiating from its centre, rather like a cogwheel – without magnification; these are almost impossible to see on the small-scale maps. So, with all these and many more mills shown in the county, which are verifiable, it's scarcely likely that he imagined the one on the Gabhra Island at Dowdstown.

On discovering the aforementioned 'new townland' of Dowdstown, in Tara parish, I rechecked the Civil survey of 1655. There, under the heading of "Castletownetaragh" (sic), I noted the following entry, "On the premisses on stone house one watermill & Divers cottages" (sic). I had found the mill shown on Larkins Map, at least a reference on paper. The site of the mill in the area known as the Gabhra Island was possibly not in the Dowdstown estate in times past, as the parish boundary probably followed the more northerly route of the river. But in our youth and at time of writing it is so, the boundary now seems to follow the more southerly course. When the M3 is constructed the line will change once again with the re-cutting of the Gabhra and much of the former 'Island' will lie buried beneath the motorway.

The symbol on Larkin's Map and the entry in the Civil survey were the first and only indications I ever had of the presence of a mill in this area, but it doesn't surprise me in the least, because of the three rivers flowing through the valley. There was once a mill on the Boyne at Ardsallagh, directly across from the confluence of the Skane. This is indicated on the 1836 OS map but is now long gone, the only remaining traces in my childhood being the eel traps, which were once part of the headrace, but these too are now gone. The presence of the mill on the Gabhra, close by what was probably one of the ancient roads leading from Tara, is intriguing and makes one wonder if this had something to do with 'the Kings Mill' of legend, perhaps it was Cormac Mac Airt's actual mill. It's closer to Tara and had a much greater supply of water than the mill in Lismullin – also, it was accessed from one of the supposed ancient five roads of Tara, reputedly the old turnpike road ran on the same course as the *Slighe Asail*. I know there's a strong body of evidence supporting Lismullin as the site of the Kings Mill, but these things can get mixed up over many centuries.

I took all these findings to the NRA archaeologists at their offices in Navan, in 2007. Some members of staff didn't seem overly interested at first, perhaps they thought I was a crank trying to impede progress. I formed the distinct impression that some of them didn't welcome input from mere amateur historians. Eventually they produced evidence from the aerial survey of some ground 'anomalies' and of the site being excavated a couple of years previously, but nothing was found. However, the archaeologists wouldn't have known specifically what they were looking for, as they hadn't studied Larkin's Map, so they were working in the dark so to speak, as this map provided the only graphical clue of the presence of the mill. But I still wonder, as I have vague memories of seeing some old mudwall ruins on the Gabhra Island, during my many trips to milk our cow over in Barney Norton's small field behind the "Teachers Cottage". The M3 route takes it across the Gabhra Island and the site of the old mill, as depicted on Larkin's Map, will most likely be buried forever. When this happens, we shall never find out anything more about the ancient mill that once stood on the little island in the middle of the fields near Tara.

About a hundred yards past the Cardiffstown stream, the road swung abruptly to the south again and started the climb up the lower slopes of Tara – this was the former location of number twenty milestone. The OS map of 1836 shows two separate dwellings on this corner, but in later years, probably in the early 20th century, a cottage was built on the site. This cottage became known locally as the "Teachers Cottage", some people say because a teacher from the nearby Dillon's Bridge School lived there for a time.

From the cottage to Castletown Crossroads is a distance of about a half mile, the road is well surfaced, the gravel lane of our childhood was tarred and chipped sometime in the 1960s, it runs between narrow grassy banks for most of the way. During our youth, this stretch was famous for the wild strawberries growing on its roadside ditches and we had many a munch of the delicious fruit whilst walking up its sloping track. This part of the ancient road looks as though it has not been altered for several centuries – and it probably has remained relatively unchanged since the times of the turnpike road. Nowadays, it is just a cul-de-sac, providing access to the "Teachers Cottage" and terminating in the muddy lane leading to the scarred field, which in days of yore was the Clooneen Wood. There's another converted bungalow a short distance up from the cottage, which is unoccupied at time of writing – in the past this was just an old stone farm building. I'm told that in former years, a man named George Graham lived here and that he was an uncle of Mr Holmes (the Deacon), who then owned Castletown Farm.

Supposedly, during the rebellion in 1798, when a large contingent of rebel Croppies were massed on the Hill of Tara, a dastardly plot was hatched by some of the local gentry and the military leaders. This plot involved sending two or three cartloads of whiskey across the hill, some say from the distilleries in Navan, others that it was a dealer named Cregan who arranged the shipment. He was said to have been paid by Lord Fingall to take the spirits across the hill, with the intention of getting the rebels drunk and not as a gesture of good will. It is also reputed that the said Lord, who was the commander of the Skryne Yeoman Cavalry, was very aggrieved by an earlier raid on his residence, Killeen Castle, and, that he was itching to get his hands on some rebels to exact his revenge.

If the story is true, these carts probably trundled along this very road and on up to the hilltop, where the plan worked beyond the wildest expectations of the plotters. The rebels seized the spirit, and it wasn't used as embrocation for sore limbs, but imbibed in copious quantities – a report from some rebel commanders stated that *"there were many puncheons of whiskey being distributed around the hillside several hours prior to the battle".* The results were disastrous for the Croppies – though they supposedly outnumbered the military by almost ten to one, in their poorly armed and drunken state they were no match for the well armed, sober and disciplined military, hence the slaughter was mighty. Thus the so-called 'Battle of Tara' was more like a massacre – it could be said that the whiskey, which was transported along the turnpike road had won the day. Like in all other battles "to the victors go the spoils", also, the said victors nearly always write the history of the battles. Hence it's unlikely that we shall ever know the full truth of what happened on the Hill of Tara during those few days in May of 1798.

About halfway along this stretch, the Cardiffstown stream runs through a deep ravine, just to the right of the road – I was told that there had once been a dam here and a hydraulic ram to pump the water up to Holme's house beside the ruins of the castle. In later years the place was used as a 'sheep dip' because of the strong flow of water provided by the old dam. The castle was under siege several times during the rebellion of 1641 and the Cromwellian campaign. I have seen it mentioned in some writings of the period, as Jordanstown Castle, but, as I believe there was no castle in Jordanstown, I have supposed that the references were to the old castle in Holmes farm (nowadays Mc Cormac's). The entrance to the house was originally from the turnpike road, up beside the crossroads – as stated, this house and farm were owned by William Holmes (the Deacon) in those far off days of our youth. I still remember him driving around on an old grey Ferguson TVO tractor, with a transporter box on the back, oftentimes going down to Cathy Robinson's shop in Garlow cross. He was a big friendly man who always seemed to be wearing an old slouch hat and a friendly smile. The 1836 OS map shows a residence on this site back in those early days when the survey was completed. On the other side of the road, is the big Rath, known as Rathmiles, the fort of Ramillies – in his writings of 1836, John O' Donovan describes this mound as Rath Lugha. It stands in the fields over near "the Boxer Daly's" farm, overlooking Dillon's Bridge on the N3 – on the OS maps this house and farm are also named Rathmiles. The Rath is a survivor of the many outlying forts once surrounding the Hill of Tara, a mound, which is overgrown with vegetation and looks rather like a sentinel guarding the ancient *Slighe* of the High Kings.

At Castletown Crossroads, the route of the turnpike is intersected by the road that once ran across through Lismullin and on to the Decoy. The remains of this being the short section nowadays linking the N3 and the Royal Tara Golf Club in the former Deerpark of Bellinter – more about this road later. The Taylor and Skinner map, the OS map of 1836 and Larkin's Map, all show Castletown Crossroads with substantial buildings in the area of the road. On the left, towards Tara is Castletown House. In our childhood, this was owned and occupied by Barney Norton's family and in earlier days it had been occupied by the Phillips family – the Taylor and Skinner map shows the road going west towards the golf club as the Trim road. On the Tara side of the crossroads, the Coachroad ran between narrow grassy banks for a couple of hundred yards, then after rounding a slight curve, it widened and started the ascent of the hill. From much viewing of the maps, I would say that it followed the path of the present day road, which has been a well travelled route in the intervening years. From Castletown Crossroads and on across the Hill of Tara, to Ballyna Crossroads, the track of the turnpike road has been in use as a public road ever since. It probably predates the turnpike era, but as there were effectively no proper road maps before the Taylor and Skinner maps, it's impossible to trace the exact route in earlier times.

The turnpike road continued on up the northeastern slopes of the hill and reached its highest level at the old churchyard gates – this is just past the green banks, which are the only remains of the ancient banqueting hall, known to some as "the house of the thousand soldiers". Just below the banquet hall, another of the fabled five roads, the *Slighe Mor,* reputedly cut across the hill from a junction off what later became the turnpike road – it wound its way across the hilltop, then headed westward over the Eskers in the midlands. Though there is nothing definite on any of the maps, there are several variation in the roadside hedges and ditches along the slopes.

There's only one dwelling on the stretch of roadway climbing the slopes; this is a cottage, which was lived in by Phil Reilly and his family, he once worked in Dowdstown. We stopped many times here for a drink of water during our walks up the hill long ago. As a point of interest, the family in those days obtained their drinking water from one of Tara's famous five wells – this was known as *Tobar Finn,* or Finn's Well and was located close by, near Grainnes Mound. In the 1830s, during the ordnance survey, John O' Donovan and his scholars called this section of the road, up near the summit, the *Slighe Cualann* and have marked it as such on their sketches. The road up the hill passes an area that historians have named "the slope of the Chariots "or *Slighe Fan na gCarpad"* – supposedly, the warriors of the High Kings had raced their chariots on these slopes. Some modern scholars seem more inclined to believe that this road was possibly the *Slighe Asail* in ancient times, which supposedly led to Teltown, of the Tailteann Games and onwards towards the mid west. Whether the warriors had or hadn't raced up and down the hill, I have no idea, but many times whilst I was training for the Ras Tailtean, I raced my humble bike up these same slopes – though I doubt that this will be recorded in history.

The summit of the old road is on the eastern side, just below the highest part of the hill, which is over near Cormacs Mound and overlooks the great vista to the west. The history of the famous hill has been well documented by many great scholars over the years; therefore I'm not delving further into its mysteries in these humble writings.

On the hilltop and opposite the churchyard gates, a road branches off to the left and descends towards the northeast – passing the once grand entrance to Tara Hall (Newhall) enroute. Supposedly this was the route of another of the ancient roads of Tara, the *Slighe Mhidhluachra, the road to Ulster.* This road ran on over what later became the route of the realigned turnpike (later still the N3) and joined the Castletown road within the Lismullin estate. The route is shown clearly on Larkin's Map but not on any of the OS maps – whilst the Taylor and Skinner map indicates the road and the Decoy, its exact route is unclear. This is useful information nonetheless, as it indicates the presence of a place named the Decoy as far back as 1778.

In our younger days, the old Inn on the right side of the road had by then become a thatched house and there was a little shop there, which was run by the Devine family. In earlier years it had been a pub and there were some great anecdotes about how it had lost its licence, supposedly this traumatic event occurred in 1911. Some said that it had happened because the local tipplers, sitting outside, had refused to doff their caps, as a mark of respect to a few of the local gentry prancing by on their horses and that they had complained to the Magistrate. Opposite the shop, and to the left of the road, the ancient village of Tarah has disappeared, but I'm told that in the days of the turnpike road, it was a thriving community of about ten houses. I believe there are some photographs of the place in the National Archives.

The turnpike road ran on past Saint Patrick's Well at a place known locally as the haw-haw, in ancient times this well had several different names including 'the well of the white cow', 'dark eye' and 'Cormac's Well'. Beyond the spring the road commenced its descent of the hill towards the junction with the road to Odder; this is also shown as the Trim road on the Taylor and Skinner Map – some scholars say this intersection is where the *Slighe Dhala* changed course and swung south-westwards. Nearby, there is a very small townland of five Irish acres or so, probably one of the smallest such townlands in Ireland – it's called Fodeen (Faudeen) and it's on the southwestern slopes of the hill. Close by, there's another of the famous wells, named Neamnach's Well (Nemnach) – supposedly this means 'the spring of crystals or the crystalline spring'. At Rathmaeve, the Skryne road branches off to the left, this is the only direct route to the Hill of Skryne from Tara and it's shown on all the maps, pretty much on the same route as it follows nowadays – though on the Taylor and Skinner map the connection is confusing. There's a road shown leading from Rathmaeve towards a castle at Skryne. It being the most direct route from Tara, this may once have been the ancient road to there, which is much referred to by scholars. It's routed through the townlands of Castleboy and old Ross (Ross means wood), and crosses the re-routed turnpike (later the N3) at Baronstown Cross (now Meaghers Cross), then over the River Gabhra to Skryne Castle.

From Rathmaeve, the route headed on past Belper Hill, with the big house and farm buildings located a short distance to the right – there was a dispensary built here sometime around 1840. Then a long straight stretch led down to Ballyna Crossroads. This crossroads, in my youth, was known to us as Ballyna Cross, but nowadays it's mostly referred to as Belper Cross. Larkin's Map shows a cluster of buildings around the crossroads, indeed almost a hamlet, and names the area as Ballyna, but I can't find any reference to this name on the OS maps. There is no indication of the crossroads on the Taylor and Skinner map, this map seems a bit confused around the particular area and is very difficult to interpret as a consequence. I have heard the crossing road, from "Big Batterjohn Cross" through Dunsany towards Oberstown, described as the old Trim Drogheda Road in those times (reference John O' Donovan 1836) – this is possibly correct, as the Trim to Drogheda road had only recently been built through Dowdstown at that time.

Apart from the short stretch of laneway from the iron gate at the Clooneen Wood, to the 'Teachers Cottage', the previously described section of the old turnpike road was used in one form or another since the old route of the Dublin to Navan turnpike road became defunct in the early 1800s. Hence its route is well delineated and there are not too many doubts about its former location – though there are still mysteries about some of the sites accessed by the road in bygone days, for instance the old mill on the Gabhra as shown on Larkin's Map. The coming of the motorway will eliminate any chance of further discoveries on its former site. I have an idea where the millstones from this mysterious mill may have gone – or at least where they were placed for some years. If you are still interested, refer to my other book *An Ancient Road in County Meath,* specifically the section dealing with Dowdstown and 'The Well of the Dishes'.

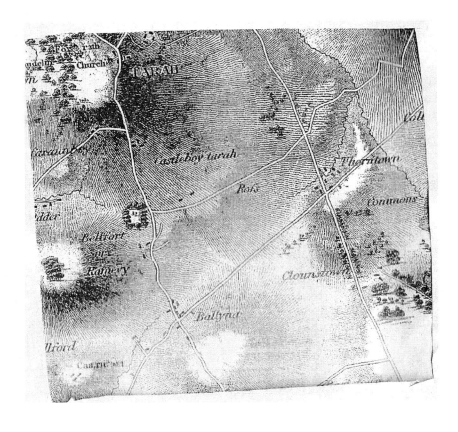

Section of Larkin's Map (1812 – 1817):

The turnpike road from Tara to Ballyna.

Chapter 7

From Ballyna Cross Through Killeen to Dunshaughlin

Though I could find no definition of Ballyna in the context of this particular crossroads, yet John O' Donovan's 1836 explanation of the same name in regards to Bective is interesting. There, he concludes that in Gaelic it means "Beal an Atha" or the mouth of the ford – but, unlike in Bective, there's no river of note in the immediate vicinity, so I fail to see its relevance for this particular place. However, there is a tenuous connection – it may have derived this name from the Bective Ballyna. From here a road leads to Bective, via Dunsany and Kilmessan, therefore the name may have been derived through local usage – rather like the way Philpotstown Cross became known as Garlow Cross. It's marked as Ballyna on Larkin's Map, but I haven't seen it on any of the other maps.

The stretch of road, from Ballyna Cross (the old spelling) to the Killeen road is known locally as "the old road". It's a narrow country road, mostly straight, and climbs its way up the hill to the old Coachman's Inn, then descends again until it comes to the 'T' junction at the Killeen road, which is the northern boundary of the Killeen Castle estate. Close by here, the number 17 milestone was located. Nowadays its southerly route comes to an abrupt end and the only choices of directions are to turn eastward towards the N3 at Birrelstown, or westward towards the Dunsany/Dunshaughlin road. There is not a trace of its former route, which took it across the Killeen road and on through the estate towards Dunshaughlin This was in fact its route, from at least around 1730, until the very early 1800s.

I'm jumping ahead again. Let's go back to Ballyna Cross and tell the story of this section, using the crossroads as our starting point. After this part of the tollroad fell into disuse following the re-routing of the turnpike in the last years of the 18th century, around 1798, the road became a cul-de-sac from the crossroads up to and beyond the Coachman's Inn. The other part of the road, from the gate that once blocked the top of the lane, known locally as "the middle gate" at the corner of O' Donohoe's field, to the Killeen road, became a farm lane for many years − here it was closed off by another gate. It was reopened as a public road in1955 and restored to its present condition by Meath County Council. Noel Devine of Soldier's Hill gave me a clue when he told me that he thought the road had been a cul-de-sac until very recently. But I remembered cycling on it many times in the 1960s, whilst training for cycle races − in fact, I reckoned I came across my first ever "free spirit" or ghost, up near the old Coachman's Inn, whilst cycling this road one very dark night. But *sin sceal eile*, a story for a little later. The riddle was finally solved for me when my old friend of my cycling days, Mickey Creighton, from Bective, loaned me the Dunsany Book, which details the history of Dunsany and Killeen from 1894 to 1994. I found a short piece therein, which describes the reopening of the road in 1955, for this I'm eternally grateful, as it provided yet another link in the chain of knowledge, which helps to join all the pieces together.

Larkin's Map and the Taylor and Skinner maps, show the Turnpike road passing through the Killeen estate and to the east of the castle – then emerging from the estate at Clavinstown Bridge beside the old corn mill. They don't show any great details of the Killeen Castle estate or what it was like during those times. Mick Kenny, the noted Historian from Dunshaughlin, had told me that the road had emerged at the formerly named 'green gates' near Clavinstown Mill, but he wasn't too sure where it had entered Killeen. This information was a great help, as it gave me a sure starting point, so I kept looking. I had been researching both the 1882 and the 1911 OS maps, but these provided very little insight, as all traces of the tollroad seemed to be erased and it appeared to have merged back into the landscape of the estate and its many avenues. Then I finally obtained a copy of the relevant sheet of the 1836 OS map and, except for a few metres, I have managed to piece together the route of the turnpike through the Killeen Castle estate – these were the last missing pieces of the jigsaw, so to speak.

The Taylor and Skinner map doesn't show Ballyna Crossroads, this is an omission I can't fully understand or explain – except that perhaps the road from Dunsany to Oberstown may not have been cut in 1778, when the map was surveyed. Though this seems unlikely, nevertheless, at the time of writing, it's the only explanation occurring to me. It was definitely in existence post 1812, as both Larkins Map and the 1836 OS map show it clearly – note my previous reference to O' Donovan's letters in which he refers to it as the old Trim to Drogheda road. The turnpike road ran up the hill and passed by the old Coachman's Inn, which stands on the left side of the road. This is clearly shown on the 1836 OS map, as is the turnpike road as far as the Killeen Road. On the map, the Inn is remarkably similar in layout to the buildings I described earlier near Kilcarn Bridge – this tends to reinforce my contention that the ruins at Kilcarn may have been an Inn. Perhaps they were built by the road trustees as part of the upgrading of the road, or possibly were of a much older vintage. The old Inn near Ballyna has been restored recently and I believe it is now being used as a residence. Reputedly, Michael Collier, otherwise known as "Collier the robber", operated his private business around this area – the said business being that of a professional highwayman. A native of Bellewstown, he supposedly marauded this area with a gang of miscreants and in later years reputedly died of a fever in his room at the back of the old courthouse in Navan – if true, it's a touch ironic.

There is nothing remarkable on the stretch of road between the old Inn and the boundary of the Killeen estate – nowadays it's just a narrow country road with hedges on both sides. It was on this part of the road that I had my ghostly experience all those years ago – if I recall correctly, it was in 1966. Towards the end of January of that year, I was out on my bike one night, training for the Waller Cup, a road race held annually by the Bohermeen Cycling Club. I had ridden up the Dublin Road, from Garlow Cross and turned right at Ross Cross – then at Ballyna Cross I turned left. My intention was to ride to Killeen, then through Kilmessan and home by Bective, just a short spin to warm me up on a cold frosty night – oh for those happy days of our youth. Passing the old Inn, (I didn't know anything about its origins then) I got a most weird feeling and the hairs on the back of my neck started to prickle and stand up. I felt there was someone or something beside me, on my left, between myself and the roadside ditch and whatever it was it kept pace with me no matter how fast I pedalled – and, I had an almost irresistible urge to start talking to the presence beside me. On and on I went, with my old flashlamp only illuminating the road in places, its weakening yellow glow barely showing the spokes of the front wheel. But I hardly noticed the waning light, by the time I got to the junction at Killeen I was absolutely terrified – but I stuck to my original route, as I was too afraid to go back, lest I might meet something worse. So I turned right and headed down the darkly wooded road towards Dunsany. As I didn't know the history of the place, I never realised I was heading for a place called the "Corp Road" otherwise known as the road of the corpse. Local legend says that all the dead bodies were carried along this way to a nearby church in olden times. In a state of terror, I turned right at the next junction and headed for Dunsany. Passing the roadside cross at the entrance to the estate, a very strange thing happened, the presence, which had dogged me since I passed the old Inn, suddenly disappeared as if by magic and everything returned to normal. I never found out if the old Inn was supposed to be haunted, but my training trips didn't take me on that road at night again. Though I cycled many miles at nightime over the years, I never again experienced anything like the fear I felt long ago on the old turnpike road near Killeen.

Today, there's absolutely no trace of where the tollroad

entered the Killeen estate on its northern side. Though, as stated, both the Taylor and Skinner map and Larkin's Map indicate that the tollroad passed through the Demesne and to the east of the castle, yet they don't show any details – their scale is too small. And for the first few hundred yards or so, the 1836 OS map shows no sign of the road, just the woods and the thickets of the Demesne. Then it becomes plain to see, heading slightly southeastwards in a curve that takes it out of the estate at Clavinstown Bridge. On its way it passes Lady Well, which is a renowned holy well, a waterfall and pond, the castle and the old Oratory. An examination of the latest OS maps reveals that, just like in Dowdstown, some of the modern avenues of the estate run on the course of the old turnpike road – though the short section that once linked up with the "Old Road" to Ballyna, is still obscured. Unlike Dowdstown, in Killeen, with all the development work in progress at time of writing, it's impossible to gain access for research and a poke around in the woods. In fact, I found it difficult to walk the adjoining roads without attracting the unwelcome and frowning attention of a suspicious security man. Hence most of my research here is dependent on the maps and some local writings. Like Tara, much has been written about the famous old Norman Castle at Killeen by many scholars, so there's nothing more I can add to this fount of knowledge. My main purpose was to establish that the old turnpike road did indeed pass through the estate and where its entry and exit points were – I think I have established these facts beyond reasonable doubt. The turnpike road through the estate seems to have been closed off sometime between 1812 and 1836, and the woods of the Demesne planted across its path.

This would tend to cast some doubts on the anecdote that Daniel O' Connell drove along it on his way to the "monster meeting" on Tara in the 1840s, though perhaps he may have taken the scenic route through Dunsany village. Some people say that the *Slighe Cualann* once passed this way, and possibly on the same route, that's definitely a story for another day – but how would one go about proving such an assertion, how indeed?

Leaving the environs of the Killeen Castle estate, the turnpike road linked with the Dunshaughlin to Kilmessan road at a forked junction, just west of Clavinstown Bridge. This is a stone arched bridge carrying the combined roads over a small stream, which some people call the Clavinstown River – whatever its name, it pays tribute to the Skane a little further south, towards Warrenstown. Crossing the bridge, which is of a remarkably wide construction, the road headed slightly to the southeast towards Dunshaughlin, just over two miles distant. A short way beyond the bridge there's a small road leading to the left. This is a narrow country road winding its way through Smithstown and on to the Glebe – it's likely that the road once branched at Smithstown and went to the east to link with the Trevet road. At the Glebe it swings sharply to the right and joins the new route of the turnpike road, post 1790s – nowadays the N3. Though I have no way of proving it, I also suspect that this road once linked up with the Killeen Road somewhere near Birrellstown – and that it also ran to the east across the N3, to link up with the small road from Collierstown to Trevet.

A short few yards up this road to the Glebe and close by the wide bridge, is Clavinstown Mill – a large four storey stone building that's still standing at time of writing. It was powered by the small stream, via an overshot waterwheel and was in working order until relatively recent times – I heard an anecdote, the veracity of which I can't establish, that it was once a six storey building and that two levels had been removed for some reason. I believe that over the years the mill was known by various names, including Mac Namura's Mill, Teelin's Mill and its present name Clavinstown Mill and there may have been some others of which I'm unaware. Unfortunately, though it's still standing, it's beginning to look the worse for wear and, like many such olden things, may merge back into the countryside, just like the ancient road, the route of which I'm attempting to confirm once more.

There were two milestones on the section of road between Clavinstown and Dunshaughlin – these were number 16 and number 15, Mick Kenny said that they were taken up about fifty years ago during road widening schemes. Another mill was situated around this area, both it and Clavinstown Mill are shown on Larkin's Map and the 1836 OS map – it stood on yet another small tributary of the Skane and was driven by its waters. This stream flowed under the turnpike road at Clowanstown Bridge, about a half mile on the Dunshaughlin side of Clavinstown – the second mill was to the right of the tollroad and a little lane led down to it from near the bridge. I heard that it was once called Devlin's Mill and it had a stone plaque depicting its date of erection, possibly in the 1770s. I'm told it's gone now, the remains supposedly demolished and replaced by modern buildings. Someone also told me that the little stream had been piped and filled in, but I'm not sure if any of this is true. Unfortunately, like many other places in the modern progressive Ireland, a set of electronically controlled gates block the old lane leading down to this mill – therefore I can't stroll down there to verify if the tales I have been told are true. I made no further inquiries, as the modernistic soap opera type name on the gate pier rather deflated my desire to inquire further and I reckoned that if people wished to lock themselves behind barriers, why should I disturb their tranquillity.

On the last stretch into Dunshaughlin, the same part known to the old-timers as "the old road", there are two roads leading off to the right. The first of these we encounter after Clavinstown is a small lane heading down to the Drumree road, then we come to the main road from Drumree. This is the present day route leading from the Blackbull to Trim road, near Culmullin – the Cross Keys, once an Inn on the tollroad to Trim and Athboy, is some distance further to the west. Before the fork of the Drumree Road, the 1836 OS map indicates a country house on the right, which was named Readstown House. The turnpike road runs on into the village of Dunshaughlin, passing the tollhouse, which stood on the site of the *Gael Scoil,* as Mick Kenny tells me. So we come to the end of this largely forgotten and unknown section of the Navan to Dublin turnpike road. From here to its final destination in Stoneybatter, though it's no longer the main road in places, it has mostly remained a well-travelled road over the many years of its existence.

The turnpike road that once was routed out from Dunshaughlin towards Dunsany and passed through Killeen then across the Hill of Tara, has faded from the local consciousness –

as all things do with the passage of time. The new line of the road, from the village to Philpotstown Cross (Garlow Cross) and later to Kilcarn Bridge, became known as the Dublin Road and, for a while it too was a section of turnpike road, until the dissolution of the tollroads in the 1850s. This major reconstruction brought great changes to the surrounding countryside – many alterations took place over the years and new place names were spawned. Names such as Ross Cross, Meagher's Cross, Soldier's Hill and Dillon's Bridge were born and have remained since – though their locations and surrounding landscape are rapidly altering, the names may possibly last for the foreseeable future. Another change forced by the major realignment was the repositioning of the Dunshaughlin turnpike gate or tollhouse. It's former location being on the old road to Dunsany, where the *Gael Scoil* was built in later years. Mick Kenny tells me it was transferred to a house in the village in the 1790s, where he later had his butchers shop. He also said that when he took over the premises in the 1940s, some signs of the gate mountings were evident on the front wall. The building is still there on the corner of the Ratoath road, having been damaged by a truck in recent years, it has been restored and is now in use as part of a solicitor's office.

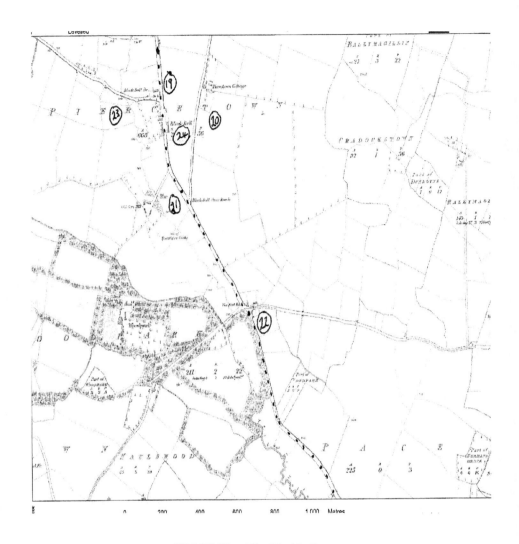

1836 OS Map: The Blackbull.

… denotes older line of road   − − − denotes newer line of road

19. Site of The Blackbull Railway Bridge   20. Site of Fairyhouse Railway Station

21. Ward Memorial   22. 'The Flathouse'

23. The Black Bull Bridge over River Tolka   24. The Black Bull Inn

Chapter 8

The Turnpike Road – Dunshaughlin to the Blackbull

One of the many notable features of Dunshaughlin is that three well known rivers rise in its hinterland, and they all flow in different directions before eventually joining up with Neptune in the Irish Sea. These are the Broadmeadow River, the River Tolka and the River Skane. The Broadmeadow supposedly rises in Saint Seachnaill's Well (Saint Shaughlin), to the east of the village and meanders its way eastwards – passing through Kilsallaghan and Swords and onwards towards the sea, somewhere over towards Malahide. In olden times, the waters of this well reputedly contained great purgative properties. Not too much imagination is required to figure out how the river received its name, probably deriving it from the many broad meadows through which it passes on its way to the sea. I have no definite knowledge as to how the Tolka derived its name – but Mick Kenny told me that it rises in the Rath Hill - Ballinlough area, to the southwest of the village and flows south-westwards towards Batterstown, then turns to the southeast and flows towards the Blackbull. It passes under the Trim road at the Blackbull, meanders through Moorepark and Dunboyne, then onwards to Dublin, where it enters the sea near Ballybough Bridge. On its winding and swampy route, two other small rivers join it at Woodpark, near the Blackbull – Mick Kenny told me that one of these is the Romany River, which rises near Culmullin (the corner of the mill or the mill of the corner J O' Donovan 1836). Mick also told me that he found some references to this river in ancient writings, stating that the name derived from the word romance. Many locals in the area contend that the river flowing from Culmullin is the real Tolka, therefore I carried out some further research, the results of which I will discuss in the section dealing with the Flathouse area.

I have my own ideas as to the derivation of the name of the River Skane – over the years I have listened to much speculation amongst scholars about its origins, some say it may even be derived from an ancient river Goddess. I think that my explanation is simpler and much more earthly. Being born and reared in its beautiful valley, I always took a great interest in this stream. As children, I, together with my brothers and sisters played on its green banks and swam in its once sparkling waters, oftentimes picnicking by the stream near the old Cluide Wood or by its confluence with the River Boyne in Dowdstown. When the rainwater barrels were empty at home, we drew many buckets of water to help with the clothes washing and to irrigate our vegetable garden in the hot summers of yesteryear.

As to the source of the name, I think the clue is in the spelling and the pronunciation of this unusual name. When I was a child, I always spelt the name as *Skein*, I can't recall where I learned that particular spelling, but it was probably from my father, who always spelt it that way. I learned that a *Skein,* was the name given by the old folks to a portion of wool, the one we always held in our outstretched arms, whilst our mother or some of our elder sisters rolled it into a ball of wool. But more significantly, I also learned that a flight of geese is called a *Skein of Geese* – especially when they fly in a 'V' shaped formation. Many a time I have seen such formations of the birds flying across the wintry sky, past our house and on up the river valley, to which I would contend they have given the name. If the maps of the area are studied, one is struck by the shape of the course of the river, from its first rising in Gaffney's Well in Dunshaughlin, until it joins with the Boyne at Dowdstown. Firstly it flows to the northwest towards Kilmessan and onwards to Bellinter. When it comes to where the Cluide Wood once graced its banks, it turns and flows towards the northeast – effectively rounding a corner, thereby changing the shape of the rivers course into a giant 'V' shape or *Skein*. I have looked up the word Skein in several dictionaries, which confirm my earlier understanding of the meaning of the word and also show that it is pronounced Skayne, the same as Skane. I could find no definition of the word Skane in the English language except that it is an area, a Province, in southern Sweden. In his writings of 1836, John O' Donovan refers to Cluide as meaning 'a corner'. In my research I have come across various spellings of the name, including Skane, Skein and Skene, but the spelling on the 1836 OS map is Skane, hence this would appear to have set the marker for the future. This is not unusual, as many Irish place names were Anglicised during the various surveys. As a point of interest, I note that the latest Discovery map shows the name of the river in both English and Gaelic – in English it's spelt *Skane* whilst in Gaelic it's spelt *Sceine*, perhaps that's where Dad learned his spelling of the name, from Gaelic? But whether I'm right or wrong, I firmly believe that the river of my childhood derived its name from the many flights of Geese soaring over its once beautiful valley in times past.

In the latter part of the 18th century, the village of Dunshaughlin was slightly different to what it became in later times. Though it was quite a large place, containing as it did a couple of hotels or Inns, a large country house, a church and school, a post office and forge and many dwellings, the turnpike road was its main feature – as indeed the N3 is at time of writing. The present route of the N3 northwards didn't exist then, just the road to Dunsany and Tara, together with roads leading towards Lagore and Ratoath. The Taylor and Skinner map also shows a road at the Dublin end of the village, which leads off towards Drumree – maybe it did in fact join up with the Drumree road off to the west, this road is marked as the Trim Road. The hotel near the old tollhouse was called the Fingall Arms Hotel – obviously deriving its name from the residents of the nearby Killeen estate, the seat of the Earls of Fingall for many generations. The Taylor and Skinner map also shows the source of the River Skane emanating from near the centre of the village. Like all the other historic places along the route of the turnpike road, Dunshaughlin has been much written about, so there's not much that I can add to this accumulated pile of knowledge.

Leaving Dunshaughlin and heading south towards Dunboyne, the first junction we meet is a laneway to the right leading to Rath Hill, 'the hill of the fort', near where the source of the River Tolka emanates. Nowadays, the number 13 milestone stands on the village side of the junction. Though battered and scarred, it is one of the few remaining signs of the old set of milestones that once stood along the length of the road. It's a very important landmark, as it is probably one of the few survivors of the original milestones placed on the turnpike road in 1733. The Taylor and Skinner map indicates that the 13th milestone was situated nearly a mile closer to Dublin in those times, which shows that the positioning has changed over the years, due to the many realignments of the road. Thus it would seem very likely that it is one of the survivors of the original set from 1733. In my youth, many of the milestones were still to be seen along the road, but over the years most of them have disappeared, being removed for road improvements and suchlike. Maybe some are still buried in places known only to locals and possibly one or two are adorning private gardens somewhere. It's a pity they have gone, at the time of their erection they merely indicated miles travelled, yet over the years I think they have gained a greater significance. Maybe they were milestones along our life's road and perhaps their very absence is a reflection of where we're going and what we are becoming.

The next road junction is to the right near Ballinlough, this side road leads off to Batterstown on the Trim Dublin turnpike road – it crosses the old stone railway bridge at Batterstown Station, which is a well preserved relic of the old Dublin to Navan railway line. About midway, there's a fork in the road, which Larkin's Map shows leading onto the same turnpike road closer to the Cross Keys. A short distance further along the turnpike towards Dublin and close to where the 'poor law union workhouse' was later built, (1839 – 1841) the same map shows a cul-de-sac leading off to the left, with a small cluster of houses at the dead end. Over the years the stretch of road between the workhouse and Rathbeggan has been widened and realigned considerably – but mostly these alterations were small and haven't made much difference to the original path of the turnpike road. On one of these realigned sections, near the workhouse, I recall a fine spring well where we often stopped to slake our thirst during our many cycle trips along the road to Dublin.

The "Ten Mile Bush" is a village in East Meath, or so it is described in some ancient writings I once read. Larkin's Map shows a hamlet with perhaps eighteen buildings – it also indicates cul-de-sac roads to both right and left, the one to the right led to a large building. The village stood on the junction of a side road leading off to the left towards Ratoath. Nowadays, a hostelry known as the 'County Club', a garage and some dwellings occupy this area. In our youth, we always knew the place as being the start of what we euphemistically referred to as 'the straight mile', or 'the straight of Rathbeggan'. The main road, from here to the next bend near the Blackbull, was just over a mile long and we could see the full stretch from either end – this being a very unusual feature in those days of crooked roads, leastwise in County Meath. I also recall that one of the milestones stood on the right hand side of the road, about a quarter of a mile along this straight stretch.

The old village of "Ten Mile Bush" wasn't exactly ten miles from any noteworthy place, except perhaps Kilcarn Bridge, which is just over ten miles distant, in Irish miles, as measured on the route of the old road across the Hill of Tara. According to the Taylor and Skinner map it was located close to milestone number

12 as measured from Dublin. Therefore, I'm not sure as to how it derived such a name – but it's a very old name, as it is clearly shown on the road map surveyed in the 1770s. During my lifetime I always heard the area referred to by the aforementioned three names or occasionally just called 'the bush'. I notice that the name is changed on the latest Discovery map, it is recorded on this map as 'the Black Bush'. Research shows that in the distant past it was also called 'the Black Bush'. The following is a direct quotation from some of O' Donovan's field notes, being written in Dunboyne and dated Aug 25th 1836 *"Ten Mile Bush (village) so called from a bush that grew (grows) there, 10 miles distant from Dublin. It is called the Black Bush in the Name Book but without authority; the people always call it 'the Ten Mile Bush' & say that they never heard any one call it 'the Black Bush' but travellers from the North"* (sic). I note the writer states that it's located ten miles from Dublin, this is a moot point and depends on where one considers the boundaries of Dublin were at the time. According to the milestones of the day, it was almost exactly ten miles from Kilcarn. The village was located at the 12th milestone with milestone number 22 (old line) being sited at the old entrance to Kilcarn Park and just to the south of Kilcarn Bridge. As the oldest name that I can find on any map is 'the Ten Mile Bush', perhaps it's an interesting insight into how colloquial usage over the years can change place names.

The next junction is shown on the Taylor and Skinner map as a crossroads, but when this is compared to Larkins Map, it shows that the road to the right is in fact the avenue to Rathbeggan house. The road to the left leads to Porterstown; this is very much the same layout as the present day, seemingly not very much has changed here over the previous two hundred years. Widening apart, the whole section of the road, which we knew as the "straight mile", appears to have been little altered since Larkin's Map was surveyed all those years ago.

When we top the little hill and round the curve on the Dublin end of the Rathbeggan straight, the situation is entirely different – here everything has changed utterly over the years and even in my lifetime. The first major alteration to the line of the road seemed to have been caused by the coming of the railway in the 1850s; this track was opened in 1862. The Dublin to Navan railway, known to railwaymen as 'the Meath Road', once crossed the line of the tollroad here at the Blackbull railway bridge, which bridge was a cast iron structure spanning the road and resting on stone abutments on either side. It was a slightly skewed crossing, running from the northwest and crossing the line of the road in a southeasterly direction.

The former line of the turnpike took it around a sharp curve, just after it topped the knoll at the end of the Rathbeggan straight. I'm told that at time of writing, this area is known as 'the Flathouse', supposedly because a nearby farmhouse has a flat roof. If true, the story lends an interesting insight into how the original Flathouse, less than a mile further up the old route of the turnpike, may have derived its name through local usage. The curve once brought the road onto a line taking it under the railway bridge, which was located about one hundred yards on the Dunshaughlin side of the Blackbull to Trim road junction. Many accidents occurred here at the bend, oftentimes caused by vehicles building up considerable speed on the unusually straight road, Some drivers seemed to have been caught napping by the sudden sharp turn and oftentimes ended up in the ditch. Because of the great number of crashes, a realignment of the road was carried out sometime in the early to mid 1960s. At time of writing, the previous line can be seen on the left and was used by the County Council for many years as a kind of lay-by or chippings store.

Following the construction of the railway bridge, the line of the Dublin Navan road (once the turnpike road) carried on under this bridge and past the Blackbull Inn, which was a couple of hundred yards from the former Trim turnpike road junction. It ran on by this Inn, passed the road to Fairyhouse (known as the Blackbull Cross), the Flathouse Inn at Woodpark Crossroads and recrossed the railway at a skewed overbridge, then on to 'the sheaf of wheat', which formed a forked junction for the Dunboyne road to the right. There was a big dip, or hollow under the Blackbull railway bridge, this being subject to flooding and caused much aggravation in those times. During my cycling days in the 1960s, one of our favourite training circuits took us past here; we referred to it then as 'going round the bull'. Sometimes by myself and more often with several other members of Navan Road Club, I frequently 'rounded the bull', pedalling from Navan to the Blackbull Bridge, then on to Trim, crossing the old bridge at Newtown and back home via Navan and Garlow Cross. It was a routine training run for us in the evenings after work, a distance of forty miles or so and I still retain some great memories of those days of my youth when we regularly 'went round the bull'.

The Dublin to Navan railway line, originally the Dublin Meath

Railway (DMR) but later the Midland Great Western Railway (MGWR), ran on a raised embankment for a considerable distance on its approach to the Blackbull Bridge from the direction of Batterstown. On this section, the railway crossed the River Tolka on a stone bridge just before crossing the metal bridge over the turnpike road. A common story told long ago was that the railway bridge at the Blackbull was the cause of there being no double decker busses running on the route to Navan. This was probably true, because, if my memory serves me well, it was a very low bridge, hence the big dip in the road beneath to give more clearance for higher vehicles. It was also said that many a carter from Cavan danced on the road in rage, not in glee, as he cursed the railway before unloading the top of his big load of hay, to allow his dray to pass through to the haymarket in Dublin.

After passing over the road, the railway line swung southwards and through Fairyhouse Station, which was situated close to the present day location (2007) of Fairyhouse crossroads on the N3. This station was used mostly as a halt, being in operation during big race meetings at the nearby Fairyhouse Racecourse. In those times many sidings were located here, these being relics of the days when the railway tracks were doubled from Drumree to the terminus at Broadstone station, prior to 1919, when the line reverted to single track operation. The sidings were used for parking 'stabling carriages' during the big race meetings, especially for the Grand National at Eastertime. As stated, the railtrack passed under the skewed stone bridge, later demolished, and ran across the Tolka again on an old iron girder bridge, then on into Dunboyne Station. When the line was closed and the destruction of the railway completed in the 1960s, the N3 was re-routed onto its present course (2007), which runs close to the original railway trackbed until near the 'sheaf of wheat', where it rejoined the old route that's now its course (2007).

Nowadays, as one drives slowly along the clogged artery of the N3, or sits in a big traffic jam at Fairyhouse Cross, there is little evidence of what was once there. Maybe it would have been better to upgrade the railway instead of concentrating all the resources and energy on a road that is now oftentimes more like a big car park – one wonders if perhaps there could be some lessons learned for the future, here at Fairyhouse?

During the 1960s and 1970s, considerable realignment of the main road and the side roads took place in the area. The skewed bridge on the main road, the Flathouse railway bridge, Fairyhouse Station and railway bridge and the famous old Blackbull railway bridge disappeared, leaving very little traces of ever being there. All these things happened in the space of a few short years and sometimes I wonder if my memory is playing tricks on me. Then I recall all those times I cycled through the hollow under the old iron bridge, passing the telephone kiosk opposite the junction, on my way 'round the bull', and I know that my memory is dead on.

As a point of interest, until I started my research for this book, I always thought that the name 'the Blackbull Bridge' was given solely to the old iron railway bridge spanning the Dublin road. Now I have discovered that the name is much older and is derived from the old triple arched stone bridge which once carried the Blackbull to Trim road across the River Tolka a short distance to the west of the junction. This bridge was probably constructed in the 1730s or even in earlier times, but it is no longer there. The stone bridge was swept away by the big floods on the 8th of December 1954, the same day the stone bridge spanning the River Skane in Dowdstown was also destroyed – life is indeed full of coincidences. A new bridge was built and it too is named 'the Blackbull Bridge', so the name lives on.

So far, finding the origins of the name 'the Black Bull' has proven to be difficult. The oldest record that I can find is on the Taylor and Skinner map of 1778, which shows 'the Black Bull Inn', but the exact location is not pinpointed because of the small scale of this map. On Larkins Map of 1812, the area is shown as 'the Black Bull', with no mention of an Inn. On the 1836 OS map, both the Black Bull road bridge and a building where the present day Black Bull Inn stands are shown – so it's reasonable to suggest that this building was the site of the Black Bull Inn of olden times. Whether or not it is the same building is uncertain, but I would suggest that this may be the case as to me it appears to be very old and the attached cobblestoned stables would tend to reinforce this belief. I have no idea as to the source of the name, but it seems to have been a common enough title given to such establishments in those days, as mentioned previously, I heard that an Inn bearing that name existed in Navan in times past.

Now we come to the vexed question of Yourell's Posting House, or Post House. Some dictionaries define a Post House as being "an Inn where mail horses were kept", this definition would suggest that the above named Posting House was a relay station on the old turnpike road, but where was it located? Local legends tell of it being situated on the Ratoath road and to the east of

Fairyhouse railway bridge – they also say the remains of the building were only recently demolished in 2008 to make way for the realignment of the N3. The 1836 OS map indicates that a house named Piercetown Cottage (Pearcetown) occupied this site in those days.

However, O' Donovan's field notes of 1836 paint a different picture, they state that the Posting House was 244 yards from the Black Bull bridge (river bridge). The following is a direct quotation from these notes. "Yourell's Posting House. In the S.W. part of Piercetown td. , 10 ½ miles N.W. from Dublin. A Public House and Posting Establishment on the Dublin and Navan road. The public house is a very indifferent place of accomodation" (sic). In my opinion these descriptions would place the Posting House on the corner of the junction of the Dublin to Navan and Trim roads. I notice that none of O' Donovans notes mention the Black Bull Inn, but they frequently refer to the name in connection with both the bridge and the crossroads for the Ratoath road. In Griffith's valuation of 1854 the name Yourell regularly appears as both lessors and lessees of property in the area. One such entry indicates that a Yourell had the old defunct turnpike house at the Blackbull leased from the Commissioners of Public Works at that time, perhaps this was the site of the Posting House, as the tollhouse was situated on the corner of the Trim road. Its possible that the Black Bull Inn may have been Yourell's for a time and became known as their Posting House, but this would not concur with the precise distance as indicated in O' Donovan's field notes. Or maybe the Black Bull Inn and Yourell's were both used as Posting Houses concurrently, this would not be unusual at the time, as the turnpike road was obviously a very busy thoroughfare down through the years. At this remove it's difficult to figure out what was what in those times and as my space is limited I will leave it to others with more local knowledge to work it all out.

This brings us to the end of the section of the road and also to the finish of my description of the original turnpike road from Navan to the Blackbull. Much of the previously described parts of the old road have disappeared completely from the landscape and indeed mostly from the public psyche also. The remainder of the road, from Blackbull to Stoneybatter, is well known and well travelled. It has also been much altered over the years, especially with the massive development around Blanchardstown and Clonee. In the next chapter, I will give a brief description of what I know of the route from the Blackbull to the number one milestone at Stoneybatter.

Chapter 9

The Turnpike Road – From the Blackbull to Stoneybatter

In May 2006, while doing some research, I drove to the Blackbull Inn once more – I had not been on the road for several years, therefore I didn't know if the Inn was still standing or if it had been knocked down and replaced by an apartment block. To my surprise and joy the old Inn was still there and in a much better state of repair than I remembered it from years ago. Now, the old Inn house and the adjoining roadside stables were in pristine condition and the surroundings resplendent with a colourful display of spring flowers. Instead of being on a busy main road, it now stands on a relatively quiet stretch of the old turnpike road. The once busy highway of yesteryear is now almost an oasis of calm, except for a few drivers using it for a 'rat run' to avoid the busy new junction. But the incessant roar of traffic on the nearby N3 gave the lie to the illusion of peace and tranquillity. I spoke to the owner of the property, a very friendly lady named Nancy Gibney – she showed me around and let me walk into the old stables. Inside I was reminded of my early years once more. Pieces of old leather harness hanging from the walls were a reminder of my old home in Dowdstown, further down the same ancient road and the many times I had helped Dad to yoke up the pony in bygone days. In my mind I could almost hear the dull thud of horse's hooves echoing off the cobblestoned floors. It was certainly a trip down memory lane – as I bade Nancy farewell, I couldn't help but wonder at the number of coachmen and hostlers who had trodden these same cobbles over the many years whilst the road was in its heyday.

Leaving the Blackbull Inn and heading towards Dunboyne, there's a little stone cross on the right hand side of the road at Woodpark. It's almost opposite where the old Fairyhouse road once branched off at an angle to the left, this was the original Blackbull Crossroads, known to some locals as "Vanney's turn". The stone cross was erected in memory of a Cavan man killed there in 1902, when his cart overturned. His name was Thomas Ward and he was a carter, who drove big drays of hay to the haymarket in Dublin, I don't know exactly when he died, except that it was sometime in 1902. The little monument is well maintained and has flowers growing around it, a nice touch to see in the hustle and bustle of the modern progressive Ireland.

Several of the old-timers have told me that the big drays of hay going to the Dublin market were a common sight on the old road, back in the 1930s. The large horse drawn wagons passed, during the day, with the Carter sitting atop the high load of hay and driving the horses. The following day, when they had delivered their load and perhaps stayed overnight in the city, the big empty drays were to be seen trundling back towards Navan and beyond. But there were no drivers on view, no helmsman on the bridge so to speak. If perchance the horses were stopped and someone looked into the body of the big wagon, the exhausted driver could be seen slumbering away on a wad of hay on the floor and hidden by the creels. The horses knew the old road so well that they could find their own way home, was this an early version of Radar? I sometimes wonder what might have happened if a set of strange horses were in the traces – perhaps the sleeping driver might have awakened in Naas rather than in Navan?

The 1836 OS map indicates that the remains of Piercetown Castle once lay in the Woodpark fields behind the monument to Thomas Ward. I have spoken to some locals who told me that in their youth some signs of the ancient ruins remained, but at time of writing, they have completely disappeared. The map also indicates the former presence of a corn mill in the fields southwest of the castle ruins – additionally it shows the track of an old dry mill race. This mill headrace received its water supply from the stream described as the Romany River by Mick Kenny of Dunshaughlin and by others as the southern reach of the Tolka. It ran eastwards to drive the mill, then the tailrace appears to have fallen into the northern Tolka. There are three rivers running through Woodpark, the northern Tolka, the Romany River (or southern Tolka) and an unnamed small stream. The two branches of the Tolka pass under the Woodpark road, flowing beneath separate bridges and coalesce downstream of the Woodpark road, whilst the un-named stream mingles with the combined rivers near 'the Sheaf of Wheat' road junction. I believe the Prestons of Bellinter once owned the Woodpark estate until the 1890s, at which time it became the subject of a disputed inheritance.

Just a few notes about the River Tolka, which might help to clear up some of the mysteries of the source of its name and its winding course through Dublin and Meath – or perhaps sow more seeds of confusion. The earliest references I can find to the river are in Isaac Butler's notes on his journey from Dublin to Lough Derg in the 1740s, in these writings he refers to the river as 'the Tolekan'. John O' Donovan in his field notes of 1836 refers to the river as "the Tolka or Tullaghanoge River". The latter name he explains as "Tullach na n – Og, hill of the youths" (sic). He adds a detailed description of the rivers course, including its meeting with 'the Dunboyne Water' near Clonee bridge. But significantly, his description includes references to two branches of the river meeting near the Flat House and says "Formerly it supplied a mill in Piercetown td., which is now in ruins" (sic). The 1836 OS map doesn't name either branch of the river, but the name Tolka appears after the three rivers have commingled downstream of the Flat House. The OS map of 1911 names the branch flowing from the direction of Culmullin as the Tolka River, whilst it also names the branch routed from the Dunshauglin direction as the Tolka River. To add to the confusion, the latest Discovery Map names only the river flowing from the Dunshauglin area as the Tolka, I can't find any name on the southern reach of the river.

As described in the previous chapter, the turnpike road ran from the Blackbull and passed by the Flathouse Inn at Woodpark Crossroads. In the 1740s, Isaac Butler's itinerary took him north on what he describes as 'ye great turnpike road' and he gives his impressions of the area as follows: "we left the Pace a noted Inn on our right, & another on ye division road to Trim on our left & ye village of Rathbegan on our right, from the bog of ye place ye Tolekan takes it's Spring, from whence passing to Clonee, Malahidert, Corduff, Finglass, Glassnevin & Drumconerath it enters ye sea at Ballybought bridge" (sic). Various conclusions could be drawn from this description of the district, in my opinion the most likely being that the Flathouse Inn was formerly called 'the Pace Inn' and another Inn, possibly the Black Bull or Yourell's Posting House, was situated at the junction of the Trim road. Larkin's Map shows the areas on both sides of the road leading east from the Flathouse, as being named 'the Great Pace'.

Being rather fascinated by the unusual district name, Pace, I researched O' Donovan's field notes on the parish of Dunboyne and found the following entries. "Pace i.e. , a causeway. This is the Great Pace. The Little Pace is in Co. Dublin". (sic). The entry goes on; "In the N. E. part of the ph.,10¾ miles from Dublin, the principal market town. It is bounded on the N. by Piercetown td., " (sic). The 1836 and later OS maps, indicate that an area to the east of what we called 'the Sheaf of Wheat' was named 'the Pace' – I have heard local people refer to the district as Pacetown. Perusal of several dictionaries has failed to yield any definition of the word pace meaning a causeway, or a clue to its possible derivation. However the name derived, its supposed meaning, namely 'causeway', is logical. The entire area, relative to the rivers, is very low lying and the construction of a causeway would seem a reasonable method of carrying the turnpike road across the swamp. Or perhaps the name is older than the turnpike era, possibly being coined in more ancient times, hence providing an explanation as to how its meaning was lost. As a point of interest, I can find no reference to this name in the Downs survey of 1646 or the Civil survey of 1655.

I'm not very familiar with the Flathouse Inn or its history, but

I recall that in the 1960s the yard of the old Inn was used as part of a film set for the RTE series *The O'Riordan's*, one of the early soaps, which was a great hit in those years. Sometimes, when caught out in a heavy rain shower on one of my many cycling trips along the road, if the heavy rain caused the roadside trees to leak, I went through the big gates and sought shelter in the sheds inside the yard – occasionally taking refuge in "Johnny Mac's pub". This was a pub with no beer, being only the TV version of such an establishment, and apart from an occasional drop of rain leaking through the roof, it was definitely a dry house. For me, this added some extra pathos to the later day song, "the pub with no beer". I'm told that from time to time, some of the scenes were enacted in McDonalds pub in Clonee, where the cast may have washed the dust and hayseed from their parched throats following the earlier activities in the farmyard, supposedly located in County Kilkenny.

In 1836, John O' Donovan wrote the following about 'the Flathouse: "In the S.E. part of Piercetown td , 10¼ miles N.W. from Dublin. A 2 – story thatched public house at the intersection of a cross road with the Navan and Dublin road. It is much frequented by carmen" (sic).

Lately, in May 2008, I visited the Flathouse, no longer an Inn, and met with Mick Connolly and his wife Kathleen the residents of the old Inn, now an elegant old fashioned house. Whilst I drank tea in the modernised kitchen, Mick regaled me with many yarns of his childhood spent in the area. He told me of the 'dancing board' that once stood by the crossroads and his memories of the great flood of 1954, when the ancient stone Blackbull Bridge was swept away. He recalled the days when he travelled to school in Dunshaughlin by public bus, when no school busses plied the route. They told me of their memories of the times, between the early 1960s and 1979, when the *O'Riordan's* was filmed in the yard, and how over the years since then, many fans of the programme have visited just to see the location. As I said my goodbyes, I could almost hear the voices of Mary and Tom O'Riordan and Minnie and Batty Brennan echoing around the silent farmyard and empty barns. Voices bringing back happy memories of the many times I travelled along the turnpike road in those more tranquil days of yore.

From the Flathouse, the road ran by Mullally's old forge, now long gone, and crossed the skewed railway bridge, a very tricky corner to negotiate and hence the scene of many road accidents during frosty weather. I always loved this section of the Dublin road, it was very picturesque, as it ran through several curves and under beech trees growing on the Woodpark side near the banks of the Tolka, a beautiful place indeed. From the skew bridge, it continued on until it came to the 'Sheaf of Wheat' junction for Dunboyne – I think this name may have derived from the time when these roads were used as a motor racing circuit. In our teenage years, my brother Tom and myself cycled up to see the motor bike races in Dunboyne, which were held annually during the summer, I think in July – there were also motor car races run on the circuit, though less frequently. Our main interest was in the bike racing and we thrilled at the great spectacle – the top rider then was named Ralph Renson and if I recall correctly, he mostly wore number one. I remember lying atop the grassy banks near Normansgrove – on those bright summer days, listening to the roar of the powerful engines, the smell of the hot tar and scorched rubber rising from the road surface as we ate our bacon sandwiches and wondered at the magic of it all. Sometimes we managed to get close and watch the machines fly high over Padeen's bridge. A few years later, a big pile up in a car race occurred near to the Clonee junction and someone was killed – after that, the motor racing ceased on the Dunboyne circuit. This is just another little flashback to some of the exciting things that happened on part of the route of the old turnpike road during my own lifetime. Which reminds me of the old euphenism "if these walls could only speak", this could well be applied to the surface of the old turnpike road, and if so, I wonder what tales it could tell?

I often wondered if the original turnpike road actually ran through the village of Dunboyne – a close study of the Taylor and Skinner map answers this question. It didn't pass through the village, at least at the time when the map was surveyed in 1778, but apart from a few slight variations, it ran on its present day course, from the 'Sheaf of Wheat', to Clonee Bridge. That is, on the line of the old road prior to the construction of the dual carriageway a few years ago. The map clearly shows milestone number 9 on the Dublin side of the 'Sheaf of Wheat' and milestone number 8 on the Dunshaughlin side of the road from Dunboyne to Clonee. This appears to indicate that the turnpike road, as surveyed by Taylor and Skinner in the 1770s, did not pass through the village of Dunboyne. I have found that the milestones, shown on this map, are the most effective way of tracing the old route. I doubt that the trustees of the road, who, at the meeting in Navan in 1733, made the decision to place the stones, realised they would provide an important means of retracing the path of the defunct road. So as well as providing information to the coachmen and travellers of the past, they are still informing amateur historians of what happened in olden times.

Let's change our direction and travel north for a while, heading towards Dunboyne from the direction of Clonee. The Taylor and Skinner map shows the turnpike road leaving Clonee and heading out towards Dunboyne, then just prior to crossing the River Tolka, it forked to the right and swung in a big curve towards Loughsallagh to the east – the number 8 milestone is shown a short distance along this curved section. The road to the left carried on into Dunboyne village – Larkin's Map shows the same road configuration. But, significantly, there's a new line shown running from just north of Clonee Bridge to Loughsallagh, this would appear to be the present day line of the road running from Clonee to the N3 dual carriageway. The differences in the maps tends to suggest that this section of the turnpike was realigned somewhere between 1778 and 1812. It would appear that over the years, some of the old line of the road from Clonee towards Dunboyne has faded from the landscape.

At Clonee Bridge, there was another turnpike or tollhouse, the third from Stoneybatter. In total there were five official tollhouses on the road over the years, the one at Clonee Bridge being established at a slightly later date than the others, probably when the ancient narrow four arched stone bridge was widened. Official tolls were collected at the following locations, Kilcarn Bridge, Dunshaughlin, Clonee Bridge, Castleknock and Stoneybatter. There are many anecdotes about unscrupulous individuals collecting unofficial tolls, and also much reference to bully boy tactics being used at official tollhouses throughout the country – I suppose that like anything else where 'a handy few Bob' could be made on the quiet, tollhouses were no exception.

The turnpike road departed County Meath and entered County Dublin just to the south of Clonee village – unfortunately Larkin's Map didn't follow it. The map terminates at the County border, so from here to Stoneybatter I'm mostly reliant on the Taylor and Skinner map to trace the ancient route of the road and my own local knowledge gleaned from my many trips thereon – travelling on bikes, buses, cars, trucks and occasionally on shanks mare. From Clonee the road ran on towards Dublin City, passing through Damestown and Huntstown, before reaching Mulhuddart – here in my youth, in the hollow, was a pub owned by the famous cyclist Bertie Donnelly, who was renowned for his exploits on the grass tracks of yesteryear. In my younger days, this was a very narrow and winding road, which caused great frustration to all its users – over the years there was much talk by officialdom of straightening and widening the thoroughfare. But it remained just talk and for many years nothing much was done. Then the new dual carriageway was built from the roundabout at Blanchardstown and all the way to Loughsallagh – thus bypassing Clonee and changing the face of the landscape forever.

The old map doesn't show Blanchardstown, but it shows the turnpike swinging from Mulhuddart in a big curve and onwards through Abbotsstown and Sheep Hill to Castleknock. This appears to be roughly the line through Blanchardstown and turning up the present day road to Castleknock, which crosses the Royal Canal and railway, though neither is shown, as they weren't built when the map was surveyed. Nowadays, the construction of the M50 has confused the picture a great deal more – the old line of the turnpike crosses the motorway to the west of the big roundabout taking the M50 past the canal and railway.

The turnpike, or tollhouse, at Castleknock, seems to have been sited where the present day road junction for Knockmaroon Hill and Chapelizod is located (Myos Pub), but there is no junction shown on the old map. The turnpike road continued on, following the perimeter of the Phoenix Park and milestone number 3 was close to the Ashtown Gate, at the top of Blackhorse Avenue. Then it followed the wall of the park, along the present day Blackhorse Avenue and down to where the "Hole in the Wall" pub now stands, here was the approximate location of milestone number 2. I would hazard a guess that this pub was once an Inn on the old tollroad. Then the road carried on to Stoneybatter, where number one milestone was located at the tollhouse, this was the beginning, or the end of the journey for many travellers on the Dublin to Navan turnpike road in those days.

Over the years, there were great plans to change the line of the road, from Stoneybatter, through Blackhorse Lane and on to Blanchardstown – one such scheme envisaged running the route along the Royal Canal and out to Blanchardstown. But none of these ideas came to fruition, possibly due to a mixture of political intrigue and great personal rivalries existing between the trustees, especially those between the Dublin and Meath contingents. Whatever the reason, the turnpike road ran on the route through Castleknock until it was re-routed in later years. The new line took it through Cabragh and on out the Navan Road along the present day line of the N3 to Ashtown. Here it ran very close to its old route alongside the wall of the Phoenix Park at the Ashtown Gate. The new line running past the Phoenix Park Racecourse and onwards until it crossed the railway and the Royal Canal on a humped back bridge close by the canal lock at Blanchardstown. About the 1820s, the starting point of the road was changed from Stoneybatter to the GPO, it ran up through Blessington Street, and through Phibsborough to Cabragh, some people say that this change shortened the distance to Navan by one Irish mile.

From Cabragh to Blanchardstown was a fine straight stretch of road and must have been magnificent for its time. In later years, during the War of Independence, Dan Breen and Sean Treacy, with a squad of men cycled in groups along this stretch of road. They were on their way out to Ashtown Cross, to ambush the British Viceroy, who was due to detrain at the little halt on the railway line near Dunsink and travel by car to the Viceregal Lodge in the Park close by. Dan, in the early editions of his book "My fight for Irish freedom" mentions the road and his thoughts about "the great road that travels through the very heart of County Meath" – I read the book in my early years and it made a great impression on me at the time. The ambush was duly carried out beside Kelly's pub, known as the "Halfway House", the contingent attacking with pistols and grenades only, as they couldn't carry rifles openly on their bikes. Though the squad of eleven men put a whole contingent of the British army to flight, they failed to kill Lord French, the Viceroy, mainly because they targeted the wrong car. For some reason the wiley old campaigner had switched to the first car in the convoy, instead of travelling in his customary position in the second car. Whilst the operation failed in its primary objective, it proved to be a seminal event in the Irish struggle for independence and helped to galvanise the movement towards national sovereignty. One of the Volunteers, Martin Savage, died in the engagement. The Halfway House was reputedly an Inn on the new line of the Coachroad – I often wondered how it derived its name and to what place it was the halfway point, perhaps it was halfway between Dublin and Blanchardstown?

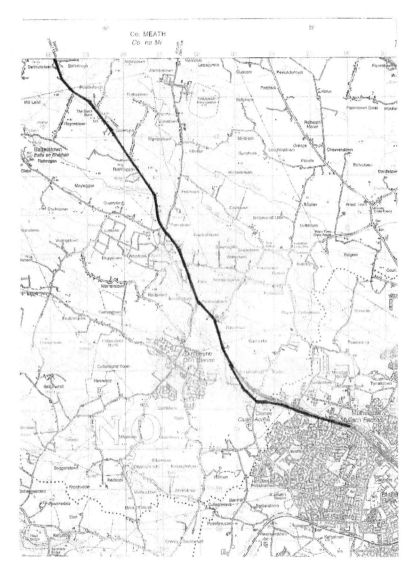

Discovery Map No. 3: Ballinlough to Mulhuddart.

The heavy black line denotes the original route of the turnpike road.

Chapter 10

The New Road – From Dunshaughlin to Philpotstown

The new line of the Dublin to Navan turnpike road was cut in the 1790s, and was probably completed by the time of the rebellion in 1798. At the time, great changes were taking place in communications and transport. The Postmaster General was gradually taking the main routes in charge, this involved both shortening the routes and levelling the gradients so that the mail coaches could cover the distances between the centres more expeditiously. Hence, the old route across the Hill of Tara was no longer suitable for the changing expectations of the times. Though the narrow winding route by Killeen and across the hill wasn't a great deal longer, as can be seen by the differences in the milestones, yet the steep ascent was a great burden on the horses. So, the route across the ancient hill was a prime target for change and the new line was chosen, being approved by Parliament sometime in the early to mid 1790s.

This realignment made a huge difference to the route, bypassing as it did the Hill of Tara, thus removing the turnpike from the path of an ancient *Slighe* and opening a new road through virgin countryside. The distance of the new line was only about six Irish miles or so, but it had a profound impact on the surroundings,

148

possibly disproportionate to its actual length. From Dunshaughlin it cut through parishes and townlands, indiscriminately bisecting some in the process. The new route went as follows, cutting through Cooksland, Roestown (Rosetown), Smithstown and skirting the Glebe, then it cut through Clowanstown and Ross, followed by Baronstown and Cabragh, it then skirted Lismullin and cut through Jordanstown and Blundelstown, before joining up with the Dublin to Skryne and Navan road at Philpotstown. All these areas, and some others not mentioned, were affected by its passage, new place names were born and a new route was opened for the local populace. Today, over two hundred years later, the path of this road is still having a profound impact on its surroundings. Some of these effects nowadays have become known around the world, with the repercussions caused by the construction of the M3 motorway through this sensitive area echoing far and wide. It's not my intention to get deeply involved in such controversies, though they have to be mentioned as they are related to the subject matter, namely the routing of the old turnpike road – strong feelings and deep passions can be aroused on both sides of the debate.

In reviewing this section of the road, let us start this time from Dunshaughlin and progress to its end point at a new forked junction in Philpotstown – later to become known as Garlow Cross. Apart from some minor alteration, the line of the new road hasn't changed a great deal over the years since it was first cut around 1796. In the early 1960s it was widened and during this period, the installation of the hard shoulder began about 1962, which in turn led to the removal of most of the old milestones. Some were replaced on the roadside ditches, but many disappeared – most of the remainder were removed later because they were causing damage to the grass cutting machines which had replaced the road maintenance workers of earlier days, who mostly used scythes and slashooks. I know of only one milestone remaining on the section – this I'll mention anon. As the road is well known and in everyday use, being at present one of the busiest highways in the country, I don't intend to do any detailed analysis of the present day. I will cover some aspects of where it will be affected by the building of the motorway and certain items of local interest along the way.

The new line of the turnpike took it almost directly north from Dunshaughlin through Cooksland – the route of the M3 will cross it just to the north of the village, heading off to the northeast towards the old church and graveyard at Trevet. A little snippet of information I recently gleaned from Mick Kenny has provided an answer to one other thing I found puzzling about the old milestones. I wondered if on completion of the new line, whether the milestones were lifted from the old part of the road and replaced on the new road. Mick said he recalled a milestone on the Cooksland section being still there in situ in recent years, a short distance from the village and in the direction of Navan. This must have been the relocated milestone number 14, which was shown on the Dublin side of the village on the map of 1778. I mentioned previously that milestone number 13 was now located almost a mile nearer to Dunshaughlin than where it was shown in 1778, hence this had a knock-on effect on milestone number 14 and all the other milestones onwards to Navan. Mick also recalls that the milestones on the old road near Clavinstown, numbers 15 and 16, were still in place then. This little gem of information would seem to indicate that the old milestones were left in place on completion of the major road alignments – but one wonders where many have gone over the years. The fact that milestones were on location on both lines of the turnpike concurrently lends support to the notion that milestone number 13 is the last survivor of the batch first set around 1733. At least that I have been able to identify – but perhaps other people know the location of some more?

The new route took it around the western fringes of a very large and famous bog, once known as "the Great Red Bog". This being a common enough name for bogs in the old days, perhaps because the luxuriant growth of heather atop the raised bogs gave off a reddish hue which could be seen from a distance. I believe the Red Bog was drained in later years and many interesting artefacts were found.

As I have previously covered the junctions of both the Glebe road and the Killeen road at Birrelstown, I will only briefly mention them here. I think they were originally part of a network of small roads and laneways bisecting the new line and some sections fell into disuse over the intervening years. On the stretch of the main road, between Garretstown and the Glebe, my uncle Finbar was killed in a road accident on Easter Monday 1953. He was cycling home from Fairyhouse races, with other family members, when they were knocked down by a motor vehicle, he was killed and the others injured. My father made a cross from a yew tree in Dowdstown and I remember Tom and I helping him to install it at the accident scene, opposite Connor's cottage, later the same year. The old wooden cross stood there for many years by the side of the turnpike road, with daffodils blooming each spring – a stark reminder of the many tragedies which must have occurred over its length down through the years.

Ross Cross was a new place-name that came into being because of the new line – though the name of the area, Ross Tara, was long established. The well known crossroads lies about a mile to the east of the previously mentioned Ballyna Cross, on the old turnpike route and it took the former Trim to Drogheda road across the new road. On the Tara side of the junction, a fine thatched house is sited, this was used as a post office for many years, but now as I write it's a crumbling ruin. I suspect the house may very well predate the actual crossroads, from its location and appearance it may have been an Inn at one stage – perhaps being a replacement for the old Coachmans Inn over near Ballyna Cross, but this is merely conjecture on my part. The turnpike crosses a small tributary of the River Gabhra just north of Ross Cross.

I heard that the road from Ross Cross to Dunshaughlin was used as part of a motor bike racing circuit. The circuit comprised of this section of the new line; it took a left at Dunshaughlin and ran across the road over the Red Bog and down to Oberstown, then back to Ross. Reputedly, the junction at Killeen Road was used as a pit stop and the then famous rider, Stanley Woods, competed in the big Leinster Trophy races, held on the circuit in 1929 and 1930.

Further north, we come to Meagher's Cross, formerly known as Baronstown Cross, probably because it's in that townland. This is where the new line intersected the road from Rathmaeve, which was possibly the Kings route to Gabhar Aichle, or Skryne. It could well be imagined as such, because the stretch of narrow winding road leading from this crossroads up to Skryne was in my youth, like a throwback to ancient times. It meandered between high hawthorn hedges growing on grassy banks and over a humped back bridge across the River Gabhra – at times it wound its narrow way between lichen covered stone walls and beneath ancient chestnut trees. Altogether, the whole aspect of the place left a feeling of medieval times upon my psyche, which has remained with me since. Now it too is about to be changed forever, here the M3 is to cut its big swathe through this once beautiful haven of tranquillity in a maddening world. In our far off youth we called it 'the old road to Skryne' and rode our bikes along it up to the hilltop, where we begged the key from Mrs Connell, the custodian who ran the little pub across from the old churchyard. Then we unlocked the entrance of the old tower in the graveyard and climbed our way up the stone steps to its top parapet. The view from there was magnificent, and we gazed around us at the pastoral scene, with the little copse of trees standing on the top of Tara dominating the skyline to the west. Yes indeed, those were great times to be young and living in such a beautiful place.

Beyond the crossroads and on the edge of the townland of Cabragh, the new line crossed the 'union boundary' – in some places this is delineated by a double ditch. Just to the north of the boundary lay a small wood or copse of about one acre, which was named Tandaragee Wood – or Toin Re Gaoith, as Gaelige, which I believe means, "the hill that faces the wind', (John O' Donovan 1836). I mention this unusual name, because in later years, in the 1960s, whilst cycle racing in South Armagh, we regularly rode through a place with the same name – I often wonder if they derive the same meaning from the name as John O' Donovan did all those years ago.

Leaving Cabragh and entering the townland of Jordanstown (supposedly named after a miller of that name), the new line crosses a little stream flowing down from the slopes of Tara and eastwards to join the Gabhra in the Lismullin estate. This little river rises over near Castleboy and carries the outflow of water from three of the famous five wells (or seven) of Tara, St Patrick's Well, Neamach (Nemnach) and an unnamed well at Tara Hall. I have heard the stream called by several names, including Nith and the Odder River, it passes close by the ruins of Tara Hall (Newhall) and an avenue was built along its banks, the entrance gates were once on the turnpike road near the little bridge. On the other side of the road, the Devine family ran a sawmill for several years, this being powered by an oil engine and not a waterwheel.

Further on, the new line came to the edge of the Lismullin estate, where a very sharp turn took the line of the road northwestward until it came to 'soldiers hill' and swung back onto its original course, almost due north. Though I'm not too sure of the reason for such a sharp curve, I suppose it served two principle purposes. Namely, to avoid cutting through the Lismullin estate for some reason and to align the road for its eventual meeting with the Skryne to Navan road, a little to the west of the present day Philpotstown Cross (Garlow Cross). As at other places, many bad accidents happened at the curve, and, during my days in Navan Engineering Works, I helped to remove some of the wrecks from the scene with the break-down truck. Like elsewhere along the road, the curve was realigned over the years until it's now barely noticeable.

The original entrance to the Lismullin estate was sited on the Navan side of the curve – from the lodge here, the avenue once ran past the main house and on over the River Gabhra at the stone bridge, to join up with the Skryne Road at the back lodge near Billy's Road. In our youth, this was a right of way and we occasionally wandered through the estate and prowled around the ornamental lakes on the River Gabhra – sometimes using the avenue as a short cut on the way back from Skryne. In later days, when the estate was divided by the Land Commission, the big house was sold off and a new entrance cut a little further up the road towards Dunshaughlin. The present day owners of the Manor House have blocked off the through way. The beautiful little drive that once crossed the Gabhra Valley is no more – though it can still be entered from either end, it's not the same. Progressive Ireland has caught up here too, with electronic gates and guard dogs being more common than the friendly greetings of yesteryear – the final nail in the coffin of destruction will be driven when the route of the M3 is pushed through this once beautiful and tranquil place.

Next we come to Tara Cross, and another junction a couple of hundred yards further on. Both of these are now 'T' junctions, with the minor roads leading off to the left, the first to Tara and the second to Castletown Crossroads and the Royal Tara golf club, the turnpike road forming the cross bar of the 'T'. When the new line was first cut, back in the 1790s, both of the junctions became crossroads – for a short time at least. From here to Philpotstown

Cross, the cutting of the new line across several roads, in such a small area, causes great confusion for someone endeavouring to retrace the old routes after the lapse of so much time. But for the help of Noel Devine, a local man, and especially the availability of Larkin's Map and some of Peter O Keefe's interpretation thereof, I would never have been able to figure out the configuration of the old road network existing in those times.

Prior to the cutting of the new line of the turnpike road, the two roads now forming the 'T' junctions, met at a forked junction a short distance to the east, in the Lismullin estate. The combined roads then ran on eastward, crossed the Gabhra and the Skryne Navan road and continued on as Billy's Road, to join the Trim Drogheda road at the Decoy. The avenues of the estate once joined this through road in several places, the main avenue joining it close to the stone bridge across the Gabhra. Noel Devine told me he had heard that the road from Tara once ran on across the estate, but he didn't know exactly where – this was the first clue and it aroused my curiosity, so I continued looking. When I first examined Larkin's Map, all was revealed, as the map clearly shows the old layout in great detail. Though the 1836 OS map doesn't show any roads, some traces can be found in the lines of the field boundaries, indeed the shape of several of the fields in the present day would tend to support the data from the old maps. I think this old defunct road is important and may go some way to solving the problems of certain mysterious old roads found in the Lismullin estate – these seemed to have been causing some head scratching amongst several historians. It proves the existence of at least another two road links between the Hill of Tara and Skryne –

I have no idea whether or not these date back to the times of the High Kings. One route, though it's longer than that previously mentioned from Rathmaeve via Meagher's Cross, runs from one of the ancient roads of Tara, possibly the *Slighe Asail*, at Castletown Cross and joins up with the old road to Skryne. The other road, as stated, ran directly from the top of the Hill of Tara and joined the first road in Lismullin. This road, where it departs the hilltop, was reputedly the *Slighe Mhidhluachra*, or the ancient road to Ulster. Therefore, I think it's significant that Larkin's Map indicates its passage through Lismullin – this in turn connected it to the road to Drogheda via Billy's Road.

About midway between the two junctions stood a police station, or constabulary barracks. It was to the right of the main road as you travel towards Navan – though it's not shown on Larkin's Map, it's clearly indicated on the 1836 and later OS maps. This may be an error on the former map or it may indeed show that the barracks wasn't built until post 1817 and prior to 1836 – but I'm sure an examination of the RIC records should reveal the truth of the matter for those interested enough to pursue it. I'm also sure these records will reveal that on the night of the 31st of October 1919, Halloween, the barracks was attacked by a contingent of the IRA from Navan and the Sergeant in charge was wounded in the ensuing firefight. The assault was successfully beaten off by the defenders and the attackers headed back for Navan on their bicycles. In his haste to be somewhere else, one of the assailants left his bike at the scene – he was later arrested because his name was found on the bicycle pump, which had remained attached to the abandoned machine. There's still a house on the site, but I don't know if this was the original police station. In our younger days a family named Farrelly occupied it and prior to that it was lived in by Biddy Grace, whom I was told once had a sweet shop on the premises – this being a great attraction for the children of the nearby Dillons Bridge School.

The old barracks stood on the fringes of Blundelstown townland – which townland is possibly named after a family of the same name (Blundell) who were heavily involved in Navans flaxmilling trade in olden times. For some reason Larkin's Map shows this area as Lunderstown, perhaps this is just a spelling error – but there is a place bearing that name near Timoole and close to Duleek. The present day Blundelstown House stands at what was once a sharp corner on the new line at the top of a famous hill, known far and wide as 'soldiers hill'. Nobody seems very sure how this hill acquired its name. Some say it was named after the previously described barracks which stood at Tara cross, but I find this is an unlikely explanation, as it was a police barracks and occupied by the RIC, who, though armed, were not soldiers. Another story, more likely to be true, is that the militia who occupied the barracks on the site of the old Navan Abbey (later the Brothers School for a time) occasionally carried out field marches from the town to Dillons Bridge, post 1798. Supposedly, they were wont to stop and refresh themselves in the Gabhra, during the hot summer days, washing their feet in the river and brewing tea. Yet another possible and likelier explanation is, that during the rebellion of 1798, when this new section of the Dublin road had been recently completed, the Navan Cavalry and Militia, used in the battle of Tara to suppress the rebels, may have billeted here close by the Gabhra. It's quite likely they were encamped by the stream, the Gabhra being the nearest large body of water to Tara; and yet a relatively safe distance from the thousands of pike wielding Croppies massed on the famous hilltop. Whatever the truth of the matter, we always called the hill by that name and I suppose it will forever more be known as 'soldiers hill'.

During my lifetime many alterations have been made to the road, it has been widened and straightened considerably. However, these are as nothing compared to the changes taking place as I write. The M3 motorway is crossing the old road at this point and a huge interchange is being constructed to link the two roads. A new network of slip roads will grace the lower slopes of Tara and shortly everything we knew will be gone, either levelled, such that it forms part of the new landscape, or underlying one of the embankments of the new road system. The little River Gabhra will be totally changed, running through concrete pipes or culverts, as one local developer remarked recently "sure that's not a river, it's only a drain" – it looks like his predictions will come to pass!

As one descends the hill, going towards Navan, over on the left near Rathmiles there once stood a fine farm dwellinghouse. Though now it's been long unoccupied and fallen down, the area is about to be obliterated by the spaghetti junction being built to accommodate the crossing of the M3 motorway. In my youth I wandered through the ruins of the old house and the remains of what must have been a splendid ornamental water garden. The garden was served by a little stream that ran on into the Gabhra, flowing by just a stone's throw away. The house was accessed by a tree lined avenue leading off the turnpike road and close by the south bank of the Gabhra – at the entrance beside the bridge were two unusually shaped stone gate piers. This was Daly's old farmhouse, I believe it was burned down sometime in the 1920s or 1930s and that the owner then was known as 'the Boxer Daly'. I have no idea how the name originated, the family then moved up and lived in a herd's house on the Castletown road. Between the farmhouse and the road a Marl bed (a naturally occurring admixture of lime and clay) is indicated on the 1836 OS map. At the bottom of 'soldiers hill' the new line crosses the River Gabhra. Much has been written about this little river in recent times – most especially in regards to the M3 and the way the famous stream will be practically wiped out as a natural river in this area. Therefore, as my space is limited, I won't add more here, because it might require a full book to cover the subject adequately.

The road crossed the Gabhra by means of a stone arched bridge, long known as Dillon's Bridge – indeed, this was the colloquialism for the entire area. Two bridges are sited close together on the same road and, just like in Dowdstown, these require quite a lot of perusal to explain why and when they were built. A mystery mill stood by the roadside, just to the northeast of the bridge, with the local national school being built there in 1860 and demolished in the early 1960s. These, together with an old post office and a Smithy that no longer exists, form an intriguing cocktail of speculation for the curious mind.

As we are moving along the road from the Dunshaughlin direction, I'll start with the Smithy. It's shown on both Larkin's Map and the 1836 OS map as just a building to the east of the road, but on the 1882 OS map it's indicated as a post office – then on the

1911 OS map it shows up as both a post office and a Smithy. From the foregoing it appears likely that a post office was located on the site sometime after 1836 and prior to 1882 – Liam Mc Carthy, a local historian who has compiled a history of the Postal Service in County Meath, tells me that the proprietors at the time were Gartlands. Then, between the latter date and 1911, a Smithy was set up on the site. Noel Devine and Elizabeth O Brien (Nee Teeny Allen), both natives of the area, have regaled me with many stories about Mary Gartland, who ran the post office in their childhood years and Johnny Gartland, who was the blacksmith in the attached forge during the same period. I recall the remains of some buildings still standing there during my youth, but they gradually disappeared from the landscape – the remains of the old post office and the forge were uncovered during an archaeological dig in 2005.

The bridge presently spanning the river is of stone arched construction and the span is about sixteen feet or so. The plaques on the breast walls would suggest that it was built by the incumbent Lord Dillon in 1860, possibly Sir John Dillon Bart or Sir William Dillon Bart, whose names feature prominently in Griffith's valuation of the 1850s. As the road was first constructed in the 1790s, over sixty years earlier, one wonders about the river crossing and what happened to the original bridge? The Taylor and Skinner maps are of no use in helping to solve this little riddle, as they predated the construction of the new line. Larkin's Map shows a bridge and buildings in the same spot as the later day site of the post office, but there is no name on the bridge. The 1836 OS map indicates a bridge and also names it as Dillon's Bridge –

however, there is one common distinctive feature on both maps, which agree with the present day topography of the area (2006). They both show a sudden change in the course of the river, taking it under the new line of the road at an angle of close to 90 degrees. This course alteration appears to be man made and involved a change of about 70 degrees to the former flow path of the river. If we follow the original line, it intersects the line of the road further on towards Navan – close to where the second, but much smaller arched bridge is located. This is also the spot where the old mill is shown on the 1836 OS map. The site of the mill and the little bridge is close to the place, where in my youth, the number 19 milestone stood by the roadside – but like many of its companions, it too seems to have vanished into thin air. Because of the sudden change in the rivers direction, one wonders if perhaps a sidestream was taken off the main stream to drive the mill – and if the smaller bridge was built in the 1790s to carry the new line of the turnpike across the tailrace?

In my youth, I recall an old swampy stream originating from close to the downstream side of the small bridge – it ran down the bottoms, almost parallel to the River Gabhra and rejoined this river at the Dowdstown Mearing and upstream of the previously described Gabhra Island. This could have been the tailrace of the mystery mill. Brendan Farrelly, a local man whose father once ran a smithy in Lismullin opposite the site of the mill farm, confirms the existence of the old swampy stream, as he recalls helping to clean it out when he worked on Donnelley's farm in the 1950s. He also remembers trodging under the little bridge when he was a pupil in the nearby Dillon's Bridge National School, in even earlier times.

Unfortunately, both the little bridge and the stream have been mostly buried by local development work.

The mill at Dillon's Bridge was just a short distance downstream from 'the Kings Mill' in Lismullin, supposedly built by Cormac Mac Airt to save his lover Ciarnat (Cernat) from over exerting herself hand-grinding corn in a quern for the king's household on Tara. Lismullin Mill was still in use during the survey of the 1830s. The unnamed mill at the bridge is about a half-mile upstream of the previously mentioned mill shown on Larkin's Map, on the Gabhra Island. According to the maps, three mills were located within less than a mile long stretch of the Gabhra – whilst a great deal is known about 'the Kings Mill' (Lismullin Mill), very little information is available about the other two mills further downstream. An excavation of the site of the mill at Dillon's Bridge was conducted early in 2007, but though I have seen some of the stone walls uncovered, I have as yet heard nothing of what may have been found there.

There's another possible explanation as to where the mill at the bridge obtained its water source – this could have come from the small un-named stream flowing from Clonardran (High lawn or meadow of the ferns J.O.D 1836) and passing under the ancient bridge at Garlagh Cross (Old Garlow Cross). Brendan Farrelly told me that in his youth, there was a dry channel running across the fields from this stream, which petered out about fifty yards upstream from the site of the old mill – perhaps this stream once supplied the mystery mill with water to drive its wheel. Then in later years it was diverted into the Gabhra upstream, near the site of 'the Kings Mill'.

Whilst researching for this book and my other book *An ancient road in County Meath,* I discovered quite a lot of information about the three mills on the Gabhra. The following is a brief synopsis.

Lismullin Mill, commonly referred to as 'the Kings Mill' is supposedly the oldest water mill in Ireland. As there's a fairly well documented record of its existence in the area since at least the middle of the 11th century, little doubt exists as to its antiquity, but whether it was the Kings Mill or not remains a moot point. Though some historians say it was located in Blundelstown, I conclude that it was located in Lismullin, the name of that ancient parish being derived from its location, meaning 'the fort of the mill'. The fort part of the name probably derives from the nearby Rath Luga. The former site of the mill is well known locally, being in an area called 'the mill farm', which is approximately a quarter mile from Garlagh Cross (old Garlow) on the Skryne road. The lane leading down from the road is clearly shown on Larkin's Map and the mill as a cogwheel symbol. The 1836 OS map marks it as a corn mill and also indicates the buildings on the site and their layout on the riverbank. Both maps show the mill to the north of the Gabhra in Lismullin townland. The Civil survey of 1655 lists the following in Lismullin, "On the premises one castle one Abbey, one Mill, one stone house & a few ashe timber trees" (sic). Griffith's valuation indicates that in 1854 the lessee of the premises was Patrick Byrne and that the rateable valuation for the mill, the house and the 26 acre farm was £36 15s 0d. The last miller was John Byrne (Christopher), known as 'long John Byrne, reputedly he was evicted in 1883 and the mill demolished by its then owners, the

Dillon family, because of non-payment of rent.

Early in 2008 I saw and photographed portion of a millstone, which was found about twenty years previously, buried on the site of the Lismullin Mill near the ancient well. There's no doubt that it is part of a 'runner' millstone, as two of the rectangular-cut drive and pivot points are visible and concentric circular marks can be seen on its concave surface. Like many such places in Ireland, one wonders what might have been found had a proper archaeological inspection of the site been conducted in the past. Now it's too late, the location of the mill is covered by farm buildings and much reclamation work has been done in the area over many years.

Blundelstown Mill has sometimes been confused with the mill a short distance upstream at Lismullin. The townland of Blundelstown is quoted by O' Donovan in 1836 as being a detached portion of the parish of Templekeeran and though bordering Lismullin it was a separate entity. About 160 statute acres in extent its northern boundary was formed by the River Gabhra. According to the 1836 OS map, part of it was located to the west of the turnpike road, extending as far as the 'Boxer Dalys' farm in Castletown Tara, with Jordanstown further south and Lismullin to the east. The mill was indicated on this map as being sited to the north of the Gabhra and close by the turnpike road, which would suggest that it was then in Philpotstown townland. The OS map shows it as an old mill, but doesn't specify its former usage. In my experience, the mill being described as an 'old mill' tends to indicate that it was disused or in ruins at the time of the survey in 1836. The river seems to have been diverted from time to time, hence the boundaries could have become somewhat elastic. I have seen this anomaly occurring several times, especially on the River Skane to the west and south, where the parish and union boundaries altered from time to time due to river diversions.

The 1655 Civil survey states the following: "Blundistown 1/3 pte of a plowland" (sic) 104 Irish acres. Under the heading of "Propriators in1640 and their qualifications" it states "Anthony Dopping a Protestant the one Moyety & William Malone of Lismullin the other Moyety" (sic). Elsewhere it says that William Malone was an Irish Papist. But significantly, in the section marked observations it goes on to state "On ye Premisses a ffulling Mill" (sic). Previously, I never heard of a ffulling mill and I thought it was a misspelling. However, research indicates that it was a word used to describe a process whereby cloth was made bulkier, or fuller, by this method. The fulling process involved dampening and beating the cloth and a material known as fullers earth was used – this being special absorbent clay which was also used for filtering liquids. I'm told by the old folk that the said Fullers earth was a well known poultice in olden times, but I have no idea what ailment it was supposed to treat. Fishermen also use this substance for treating their fishing lines and I have heard of its usage in dyeing cloth. It seems that the common surname Fuller, probably derived from this occupation.

If the Civil survey is to be believed, there was once a textile mill at the roadside near Dillon's Bridge. This should not be confused with a flax 'scutching mill', such mills being used in the early part of the linen making process to beat the fibres from the flax plants. The fulling process was used much later, seemingly following the weaving, as all the descriptions I have read mention cloth fulling. An interesting aspect of the textile mill at Blundelstown is that the townland name is probably derived from the family name Blundell – a family of this name became very prominent in the flax milling industry around Navan in later years. Perhaps the little mill on the Gabhra was one of their first enterprises in textile manufacture. I doubt if we will ever know for sure, as one of the slip roads of the Blundelstown interchange is being built over the site of the ancient mill at time of writing.

I have already mentioned the third mill on the Gabhra, namely the mill at Castletown Tara, for which I have discovered references in the Civil survey of 1655 and the cogwheel symbol on Larkin's Map of 1812, these are referred to previously in the section on the Clooneen. I have no doubt that three mills once existed on the famous little river and that two of them have been lost in history. Folklore in the area states that a mill also existed at Newhall (Tara Hall) at one time and that this may have been 'the Kings Mill' of legend. Some local people told me that in older times they saw the remains of a mill on the little River Nith, a tributary of the Gabhra, but I can find no record on the maps or in any of the surveys.

During my many cycling trips along this section of road, I noticed that there was a small hump at the spot where the little bridge is located, as well as a second larger bump at the main bridge. I never realised that the first hump was in fact a bridge, until Noel Devine pointed it out to me, hence the value of local knowledge and youthful memories is once again emphasised. At this remove, it's almost impossible to ascertain what exactly happened at Dillon's Bridge over the years and the sequence of events occurring before and since the cutting of the new line in the 1790s. But we can hypothesise and perhaps come close to a fairly accurate assessment of events.

I would speculate that at the time of the construction of the new line of turnpike in the 1790s, a mill existed in the spot as shown in later years on the 1836 OS map – access to this mill could have been from the nearby Skryne-Navan road. The smaller bridge was built to carry the new road across the tailrace of this mill. The water supply could have been derived from at least two sources, number one being the little stream from Garlagh Cross and number two being a sidestream from the Gabhra, from somewhere upstream of the bridge.

The fate of the first bridge, built in the 1790s to carry the new line of turnpike across the Gabhra, remains a mystery. Perhaps it was only a wooden structure and rotted over the years, or maybe it was stone arched and carried away in some flood – possibly we shall never know now? There are many things that could have happened, maybe some further investigation of the Grand Jury presentment records of those years will yield up more information. As stated, some of this is purely hypothesis, but just like in Dowdstown, there must be some logical explanation as to why two bridges were built to carry a straight section of road across just one river.

The National School was built in 1860. It was the local school for almost one hundred years, being closed in 1957 when a new School was built nearby in Lismullin, on the Walterstown road.

The new school replaced both Dillon's Bridge School and the National School in Walterstown. The old building was part of the property of a local farm, originally occupying most of Philpotstown townland and at the time owned by Reids (Reads), then later by Donnelly's. It was in poor repair and demolished in the early 1960s. The old schoolhouse being located on the downstream side of the bridge and up close to the river – lately, the ruins were excavated and recorded. Though the schoolhouse is gone and the bridge may soon meet the same fate, the district name is likely to remain for a long time – just one more name created by the cutting of the new line of turnpike road through this part of County Meath.

Further on, the new line of the turnpike met with the Skryne to Navan road – according to Larkin's Map this was a forked junction. The combined roads ran on through the Dowdstown estate and continued to do so for almost another twenty years. They joined with the original line of the Dublin to Navan turnpike in Dowdstown, and carried on along the old roadbed to Kilcarn. Philpotstown Cross was then in embryo form, but not yet a fully fledged crossroads – its evolution to that status will be covered in the next chapter.

I have many memories of my youthful days, when I frequently cycled the then modernised version of this road, but I have one abiding memory. In 1966, the first stage of the Ras Tailteann was a time trial, which started at Ashtown in Dublin and took the route to Navan; therefore we rode along the full length of the new line. As we swept down 'soldiers hill' and crossed Dillon's Bridge, a big welcoming sign had been painted on the road near the little hump and a huge crowd gathered at Garlow Cross to cheer us on. This is but one of the many fond memories I retain of the road, which was once the new line of the Dublin to Navan turnpike road.

Chapter 11

Philpotstown Cross (Garlow Cross), Its Origins and the Road to Kilcarn and Navan

Larkin's Map indicates the new line from Dunshauglin joining up with the Skryne to Navan road at a forked junction – this junction was a little to the west of the present day crossroads. The problem with the map is that it's dated 1812 and it shows both road configurations, including the new line of the Trim Drogheda road and Dowdstown Bridge, which weren't completed until several years later. As a result, the many road formations can be pretty confusing at first glance. Peter O Keefe, in his book "the Dublin to Navan Road and Kilcarn Bridge", has concluded that Larkin's Map wasn't in fact published until 1817, when most of the new road alignments in the area had already been completed. This explanation solves the conundrum and as a result the map can be more easily interpreted.

The 1836 OS map isn't much help in deducing the series of road alterations that finished up as the modern day Philpotstown Cross, as the crossroads was already in existence when the map was surveyed. It does show some buildings sited a couple of hundreds yards to the west, where Larkin's Map indicates the Dublin to Navan and Dublin to Ratoath and Skryne roads meeting, and the combined road running on a course through the Dowdstown estate. Hence it's a good confirmation as to the veracity of Larkin's Map. It also shows the remains of an old road heading towards the previously described road junction by Dowdstown Churchyard.

There are many local jokes and legends about the 'characters' living around Garlow Cross and the antics they got up to over the years. I can recall the groups of men and boys playing 'pitch and toss' at the crossroads in the days of my far off youth, I also heard about the crossroad dances that took place there in days of yore. But what I remember the most are the old 'pisoiges' about the legendary Saint Patrick and some of the things that reputedly happened to the Saint on his famous journey from Slane to Tara, supposedly to attempt to Christianise the pagans on Tara. The following are some of the stories I heard over the years.

St Patrick was on his first trip to Tara, to see the High King. The Saint was travelling along the main road and he came to a crossroads where a bunch of men were playing 'pitch and toss'. As he was a bit lost, he asked for directions, saying, "my good men, can you direct me to Tara". The reply he got was unprintable, but went something like this – "Ah f*** off you hairy ould b******", to which Patrick replied, "well, at least I know I'm in Garlow Cross" and proceeded on his way with dignity. Another yarn about Garlow Cross went as follows: when St Patrick was passing the crossroads he decided to have a rest and sat at the bottom of the wall, where he fell asleep. When he awoke from his slumber, he found that someone had stolen the laces from his sandals. Whereupon the good Saint lost his rag and laid a curse on the place, saying "that forever more there would be a thief at Garlow Cross"! Yet another yarn was told that when St Patrick was travelling to Tara from Slane, he walked through Navan and Kilcarne but he 'ran' through Garlow Cross.

Sadly, these are just colloquial yarns, they couldn't have happened at the crossroads nowadays known as Garlow Cross (Philpotstown), as it wasn't in existence at the time the venerable old Saint passed by – and didn't exist, as we know it, for almost another fourteen hundred years. Maybe the stories were told about Garlagh Cross (Old Garlow Cross), which is just a short distance over the Drogheda road? Or perhaps they happened at the ancient crossroads by Dowdstown Churchyard – when the Saint was making his way along the legendary *Slighe Cualann* or *Slighe Asail,* in his first attempt to convert the 'hard men and women' of County Meath.

Larkin's Map shows the road passing into Dowdstown and running to the east of both the old church and Dowdstown House. This would appear to suggest that another realignment of the road took place within the confines of Dowdstown and it was probably concurrent with the new road from Dunshaughlin. The Dublin to Navan turnpike road possibly ran on this route for a few years, from the 1790s until 1817, when the new line from Philpotstown to Kilcarn was opened. This would have fitted in well with the logic of the times, as it both shortened the route and provided a lesser gradient for the course of the road. The change in the route, to the east of the old church, effectively bypassed the steep gradient of Dowdstown Hill, so I would strongly contend that both the 1836 OS map and Larkins Map are correct, though they appear to contradict each other. A few years ago, there was some evidence in the topography of the Dowdstown estate suggesting that this was indeed the case, but the ravages of farming and the destruction of trees, old ditches and suchlike have mostly eradicated these signs now. In my opinion, there is a possibility that the road once ran through the college wood, along by the new "priests graveyard", then between the front of the boiler house, the handball alleys and the rear of the old garden. I reckon that part of the present day 'cow pass' is built over the old road and that it rejoined the old line by the north fork in the avenues. This 'Y' junction can be plainly seen in the field and tractors are driven on it regularly. The 1836 OS map shows a row of trees curving from the corner of the "priests graveyard", across where the college football fields were later sited and on towards the avenue near the handball alleys, this is the likely route of the road, as shown on Larkin's Map.

Starting at the newly formed Philpotstown Cross (Garlow Cross), we head north down the new road, towards Kilcarn, which is just over two Irish miles distant. Larkins Map shows no buildings at the new crossroads, just the previously mentioned building at the old forked junction. The 1836 OS map indicates both the farmyard buildings and the dwellinghouse, which was then possibly owned by Doppings (Doppines) and later became Reads farm, then in our youth, the house was Miss Robinson's residence and shop. The post office was sited here from the early 1940s until Miss Robinson retired in the 1970s. As stated, it also shows the buildings at the old forked junction, but there is no sign of the actual junction. There are several buildings shown on the southside of the road to Dowdstown Bridge.

This new line of road ran as straight as an arrow shaft, from the newly formed crossroads to the top of the hill at Kilcarn Lodge, which was in later days known as "The Kennel Hill" and later still as "Barry's Hill". It cut through the townlands of Philpotstown and Dowdstown and then bisected Kilcarn. Part of the Dowdstown estate was to the east of the new road, between it and the Yellow Walls Lane, which formed the boundary between Dowdstown and Corballis.

Leaving Philpotstown Cross, the new line to Kilcarn climbed the hill where the Tara Service Station is located at the time of writing, some buildings are shown on the old maps in the 'wood field' to the left of the road. The line was cut through the Fox Covert, a large wood, which in our youth ran from here and all the way over to the Yellow Walls Lane, then along the lane to the Follistown River, at the little bridge near "Cristy the Shed Mc Grath's" cottage. This stream formed the Mearing, or boundary, between Dowdstown and Kilcarn. The 'front avenue' at Dowdstown was built sometime between 1817 and 1836, as it's not indicated on Larkins Map but is clearly shown on the OS map. The gatelodge doesn't appear on the 1882 OS map, but it's there on the 1911 OS map, so it was built somewhere between these dates, probably around 1890. The entrance gates here have some history attached to them, I heard a story that they won some award at an exhibition in Paris, France, but I don't know the date. They are obviously very old; being constructed of wrought iron and riveted together and having two coats of arms emblazoned on metal plaques. In my youth, the big stone ball atop the southernmost pier was hit by lightening, I recall its shattered remains lying on the ground at the time – in later years, if I recall correctly, it was replaced by another ball made of concrete.

The number 20 milestone once stood on the new line, about twenty yards on the Navan side of the lodge gates, Dan Norton, who was an overseer on the County Council, tells me it was shifted in 1962, when the hard shoulder was first built on this section of road. Presently it's placed inside the gates and acts as a gate stopper for the southern half of the gate. The stone is in perfect condition, it indicates the distance to Dunshaughlin is 6 Irish miles and the distance to Navan is 3 Irish miles – the number 20 is carved on the side. I think it's the only surviving milestone on any part of the new lines from Dunshaughlin to Kilcarn – but I wonder how long more it will survive the ravages of progress?

A couple of hundred yards on the Navan side of the avenue gates, in olden times, a small lane ran off northeastwards across the northern part of the estate – from the line of the new road to an old quarry once sited along the Follistown River. In my youth, some traces of this lane and the quarry were to be found, but most of these disappeared with the bulldozing of the area in later years. The quarry lane can be seen clearly on the 1836 OS map.

There is only one bridge on the new road between Philpotstown Cross and Kilcarn. This is the stone arched bridge spanning the Follistown River, the Mearing between Dowdstown and Kilcarn. I believe this Mearing is to become much more significant than the boundary between two townlands, as it's soon to become the outer boundary of the town of Navan. A short distance further on, the new line bisected the old Drogheda Road, as indicated on the Taylor and Skinner maps – the remaining section of this old road became known as the Yellow Walls Lane. Both the 1836 OS map and Larkin's Map, indicate that this road once connected to the old main road and that there was a small cluster of houses where it joined with the old route of the Dublin Navan turnpike, near Brian Boru's Bridge, opposite Ardsallagh. They also clearly show where the old byroad was crossed by the new line of the turnpike. The cut off section has disappeared completely; it once ran across Major O' Kelly's field, about where Husband's cottage was built in later years.

The next significant area on the line of road is a new lane, cut to provide an entry to the mill at Upper Kilcarn. As stated, this lane became known locally as Mongey's Lane and some people still refer to it by that name. Next, the new line skirted the edge of the small wood surrounding the big house in Upper Kilcarn, at time of writing this house is owned by Miss Pat' O' Kelly – in recent years, the old house was demolished and a new one built on the same site. The new road then cut off Pastor Phillip Barry's laneway up to Pastor Hill and Oldtown – this also effectively removed the lanes connecting both Lower Kilcarn Demesne and the Kilcarn graveyard from access to the Dublin Road. Nowadays there is only a short section of the Kilcarn cemetery lane remaining and many people wonder where it once led. Most of the remainder of this network of lanes and avenues has disappeared, but there are a few traces to be found if you know what you're looking for.

I recall the number 21 milestone (new line number), which stood on the grassy bank at the roadside, about one hundred yards south of the new lodge at Kilcarn Park – it disappeared several years ago and though I have searched in the long grass in the field and by the roadside, I couldn't find any trace of it. The original part of the new lodge was built of stone and brick, the plaque above the door is dated 1888, so I presume that's the year it was constructed. It's sited on the line of the old avenue, which ran down to the former turnpike road, now Mill Lane. As stated, the original lodge that once stood by the old line of the turnpike road disappeared long ago. The plaque above the door of the new lodge has an inscription reading FOM, which I'm told, is an abbreviation of certain Latin words – there is an old story about this inscription and how the residents of the lodge came to know its meaning. One day, many years ago, a tramp known locally as "the hairy bowsie" called to the house and knocked. When the door opened, he was greeted by a very cranky person, and upon requesting alms was told in no uncertain terms to depart forthwith, in other words, to buzz off and beg elsewhere. Whereupon he pointedly gazed up at the plaque above the doorway and asked, "do you know what FOM stands for"? The cranky person, though still angry, had his curiosity aroused and replied in the negative – so the old tramp retorted, "well", he said, "it's in Latin and it means peace and hospitality to all, neither of which you have shown me today", and with that he slouched out the gate in high dudgeon. I have no idea if in fact this is the meaning of the inscription on the plaque, but I heard my father telling the story several times when I was young.

So we come to the end of the new line from Philpotstown to Kilcarn, the new road rejoined the old turnpike at the little grass triangle, once sited at the junction of Mill Lane – the spot where 'the fiery Devil' appeared to the drunk, one dark midnight back in the 1960s. As mentioned earlier, I'm convinced the Kilcarn tollhouse was originally located either at Jack Sarsfields "swamp villa", the old Coachouse (now Kinsella's house), or at the hostelry, the ruins of which stood a short distance to the south, in the field. With the changing of the line of the road, I think the tollhouse, or turnpike, may have been relocated on the other side of Kilcarn Bridge, at the building now known as the Old Bridge Inn, refer to my earlier mention of the entry in Griffith's valuation of 1854.

Now we come to the last section of realigned road, from Kilcarn Bridge to 'the skelp', the end of the line so to speak. I'm not too sure as to when this short section was cut – it's less than one Irish Mile long, but for me it was the final piece in the jigsaw of the old turnpike road. Both Larkin's Map and the 1836 OS Map, indicate that it was in existence at their respective dates, so it's reasonable to propose that it was cut at the same time as the section from Philpotstown Cross to Kilcarn. Therefore, using this logic, it would seem to have been opened around 1817. This re-routing took away the steep hill of the old road and removed 'the Swan Inn' from the main route – the 'old road' became a secondary road and many houses were constructed on its verges throughout the intervening years. One bridge was built on the new section, a small arched structure to carry the road over an unnamed stream flowing down from Balreask (the town of the mire or swamp) to the Boyne, close to Kilcarn Bridge. Then at the far end, where the new line joined the old, near 'The Swan', there's a little hill, which is known as 'the skelp'. Nobody seems too sure of the origins of this name, but I would hazard a guess that the explanation is simple and stems from a colloquialism. It was common enough, that if somebody wished for a piece to be cut off something, to issue an instruction saying "take a skelp out of it". This expression was also used in terms of giving someone a slap or "hitting them a skelp" and I heard it being used during my childhood. So I would hypothesise that this may have happened back around 1817. Somebody decided to take a skelp out of the side of the hill to allow a more level passage for the new line of the road and probably issued instructions to that effect – the name has stuck until the present day. In fact, if the whole new section, from here to Kilcarn, is examined closely, it will be observed that most of the new line was cut out of the hillside of the western side of the Boyne. Therefore at one time, the entire section could have been known as 'the skelp'.

Chapter 12

The Turnpike Road – Roads and Their Significance

Those childhood days we spent playing by the roadside were very special and provided us with a rich lode of memories. In rural parts in those times, life was very simple and excitement was scarce, so in some ways we were easily amused. The roadside was our contact with the outside world, that great unknown place we had heard so much about but had seen very little of at the time. The simple dusty country road of our childhood, where we played our games and watched life pass by, was in the future to become our escape route to this great other existence. A highway that was to take us far away from all the things and the people we loved so much. But we didn't know this then, so we played our simple games and dreamed our dreams, there by the roadside in Dowdstown, so long ago.

The foregoing is an excerpt from a book of childhood memories that I have recently written – it's a reflection of my thoughts on the subject of the local roads in the area during those far off days of our childhood, when everything was so different.

This synopsis could just as readily been applied to anywhere in Ireland, in the earlier times of which I wrote, most especially in rural communities. At the time, motor transport was pretty rare and some of the roads could be used as a play area – this we often did, playing skittles, hopscotch and marbles almost at will, then stepping onto the grass verge when the rattle and hum of an approaching car or lorry disturbed our tranquillity. Many people walked or cycled then and often greetings were exchanged as one travelled around, so a trip along the roads could sometimes be a social occasion. This was especially so at the local crossroads, where people met whilst waiting to catch a bus to town or to the city – and in the summer evenings, the 'good boys' gathered for a game of 'pitch and toss', the Devil's game, as it was described from the pulpits. Whilst it wasn't exactly De Valera's image of the perfect Ireland, with comely maidens dancing at the crossroads, it was real though, and I remember it. In the 1960s things began to change, as prosperity came creeping over the horizon and our country roads developed apace, with the traffic increasing – at the time, though children couldn't play as much on the roads anymore, yet people could still walk and cycle on them in relative safety.

Over the years since then, things have changed utterly, prosperity brought many changes to society and some of the roads have developed into mighty highways. Equally they have become death traps for the unwary, with many people being killed and maimed each year. If you have a spare half tour or so, it's well worth your while to sit by the roadside on the N3 near Philpotstown Cross, or for that matter any other main road, and watch the traffic passing. Nowadays, this road has become scary, even to view from the verge, in some ways it's a microcosm of modern Irish society – a veritable nightmare in the making, and almost like a feeding frenzy, with road rage, bad manners, arrogance and intolerance shining out for all to see. Is this a true representation of the modern progressive Ireland, is this what we are becoming and

182

if so, is it really what we want to be?

Years ago, when I moved down to live in Cork, I settled outside a village a few miles from Cork City – the main Dublin to Cork road ran through another village close by and a bypass was being built. This was a big dual carriageway; in fact a motorway in everything except name, and it passed between our new house and the local village. Things were great for a while, the kids could ride their bikes on the new road and we regularly used it for our Sunday walks, we could come and go as we pleased. Then it opened for business and soon the roar of heavy traffic became the dominant sound in the area, instead of the melodious music of the birds. No longer could we walk the fields and cross over the roads at will, now we had to look for a bridge, in essence, the new road really became a big wall preventing free movement around the rural areas.

When I heard that the M3 was to be constructed through the Gabhra Valley and Dowdstown, though I was amazed at the decision, I knew what to expect from previous experience elsewhere. I have no problems with the motorway itself, this is all part of the price to be paid for perceived progress, but I was very surprised at the route chosen and I wondered what Machiavellian hand was at work. I have grave doubts about the necessity for the vast array of new secondary feeder roads and their extent, for instance the Blundelstown Interchange and the re-routing of the Trim Drogheda Road at Dowdstown. These two road systems will in themselves completely alter the whole aspect of the lovely valley; such that it will in future be more likened to a concrete jungle rather than an appropriate backdrop to the Hill of Tara.

Whereas the delicate touch of a skilled surgeon, using a sharp scalpel, was required for such a serious operation, yet the NRA, that faceless and powerful group, seemingly assaulted the Irish countryside as though it was an enemy in battle, rather than a patient. Using an approach more suitable to a gladiator than a surgeon, they have attacked the pastoral landscape with the broadsword and the battleaxe, eviscerating and cleaving it from end to end in a display of breathtaking insensitivity verging on arrogance, backed by apparently unlimited power and a bottomless purse. Perhaps future generations will wonder how we in our generation allowed such wanton destruction of part of their heritage, the once beautiful landscape of Ireland.

Then there's the creeping development that goes hand in glove with road and other construction. Who ultimately gains possession of the many acres of surplus land acquired throughout Ireland for construction of the Motorways and what will be its usage in the future? This is but one of the many questions which might be posed at future tribunals of enquiry. I recently listened with some irony to the minister for the environment stating he would ensure that there would be no industrial development along the line of the M3. This statement makes me wonder if he ever leaves his comfortable cocoon, does he not consider a huge sewerage works to be an industrial development? The said sewerage plant flew in under the level of the radar, when the furore about the route of the M3 Motorway was at its height and whilst many people were distracted by it – which also leaves me wondering if this was part of the planning. There are huge moneyed interests involved in both projects and many future developments depend thereon – these won't be easily gainsaid. I heard one such interested person remark recently in a heated discussion, quote, "if I had my way, I'd bulldoze the whole f****** Hill of Tara into the sea at Laytown and build a new road over the rubble", unquote. I'm afraid that with such sentiments around, local opposition and history lovers never had a chance of success in changing the route.

In the dark recesses of the Limekiln wood in Dowdstown, lie the crumbling remains of Brian Boru's Bridge – together with a fair stretch of the old Dublin to Navan turnpike road, an ancient Limekiln, a quarry and an old well. All of these are immediately adjacent to a lime-encrusted stream meandering through a wooded glen. There is absolutely no doubt that this is the remnant of the said road and the bridge carrying it across the small river forming the Mearing between the ancient parishes of Dowdstown and Kilcarn. There is also strong evidence that the turnpike road was built over a more ancient route, possibly the *Slighe Asail* or some such legendary road associated with Tara. Yet the whole place is falling further into decay, with the remains of the old road almost totally overgrown and part of the bridge collapsed. In the few years since my childhood, the difference is remarkable – where once we drove the pony and cart with complete ease, now one would require the assistance of a machete to gain access on foot. Surely, here we are presented with a unique opportunity to preserve something of our recent past and maybe spend some of our supposed newfound riches in doing so. The place has great possibilities as a small theme park, and who knows what might be found if an archaeological dig was conducted here? Perhaps some evidence might be found indicating that it may indeed have been an ancient *Slighe,* after all, the place has remained almost untouched since the road ceased to be a main thoroughfare almost two hundred years ago.

In conclusion, as previously stated, the M3 makes its final crossing of the ancient tollroad, the Dublin to Navan turnpike road, in the river field behind the house where I was born and spent my childhood – it's cutting a wide swathe through what was once my field of dreams. The original tollroads were planned to last for a few years, just a short spell to help raise the standard of the Irish roads. This short spell lasted almost one hundred and thirty years, from 1729 until 1856 – I wonder how long the next tollroad will last and is it destined to be a failure like its predecessor? I also wonder if a plaque or one of those hideous metal monstrosities, we see adorning the countryside, will commemorate the crossing place in Dowdstown. Somehow I doubt it. After all, who wants to be reminded that one of the ancient *Slighte* is probably buried forever beneath thousands of tons of earth and concrete, in Dowdstown, at the place where toll roads meet?

Bibliography

My principle sources of reference for this work are the following:

- Taylor & Skinner Maps 1778 – 1784
- Ordnance Survey Map of 1836
- Ordnance Survey Map of 1882
- Ordnance Survey Map of 1911
- William Larkin's Map of 1812 – 1817
- John O'Donovan's Letters and Field Notes (1836)
- Peter O'Keefe's Book *The Dublin to Navan Road & Kilcarn Bridge*
- Moll's Map of 1714
- Petty's Map of 1683
- The Longfield Estate Maps of Kilcarn and Dowdstown (1822)
- The Downs Survey of 1645
- David Broderick's book *The First Toll Roads* (2002)
- L. J. Steen's book *The Battle of the Hill of Tara 26ᵗʰ May 1798*
- Michael Slavin's *The Book of Tara*

THE FOLLOWING IS A COMPILATION OF OLD
PICTURES AND PHOTOGRAPHS TAKEN BY THE
AUTHOR ALONG THE ROUTE OF THE FORMER
TURNPIKE ROAD

THE OLD TOLLHOUSE (TURNPIKE) AT KILCARN IN THE EARLY 1900s.

KILCARN BRIDGE CIRCA 1945.

DOWDSTOWN HOUSE.

VIEW FROM DOWDSTOWN HILL, WHERE THE TURNPIKE ROAD SWEPT DOWN TO THE RIVER SKANE. THE ROUTE OF THE M3 MOTORWAY RUNS IN THE BACKGROUND.

SIR WALTER DUFF'S CHURCH (OLD DOWDSTOWN PARISH CHURCH), BUILT CIRCA 1188.

**SITE OF ANCIENT CROSSROADS NEAR CHURCHYARD IN
DOWDSTOWN (THE CROSS GATES).**

"THE RAM" AND DOWDSTOWN AVENUE, WHERE THE TURNPIKE ROAD CROSSED THE TWO STONE BRIDGES.

THE "NEW" BRIDGE THAT REPLACED THE OLD STONE BRIDGE ON DOWDSTOWN AVENUE DEMOLISHED BY THE GREAT FLOOD OF 1954.

DOWDSTOWN BACK AVENUE BUILT OVER THE TURNPIKE ROAD.

THE TURNING ARC AT DOWDSTOWN BRIDGE, WHERE THE TURNPIKE ROAD CROSSED THE RIVER SKANE.

THE CONFLUENCE OF THE SKANE AND GABHRA RIVERS AT DOWDSTOWN BRIDGE.

THE APPROXIMATE ROUTE OF THE "CAUSEWAY", WHICH CARRIED THE TURNPIKE ACROSS THE RIVER FIELD IN DOWDSTOWN (AS INDICATED BY THE BLACK MARK). THE M3 MOTORWAY WILL CROSS THE OLD TURNPIKE ROAD ABOUT MIDWAY ALONG THE BLACK-MARKED SECTION. THIS IS THE EXACT SPOT WHERE "THE TOLL ROADS MEET". THE HILL OF TARA IS IN THE BACKGROUND TO THE LEFT.

THE AUTHOR'S CHILDHOOD HOME, A FORMER TIED HOUSE TO THE DOWDSTOWN ESTATE, ALONG THE ROUTE OF THE TURNPIKE ROAD, WITH A VIEW OF THE HILL OF TARA IN THE BACKGROUND.

THE FORMER TEACHER'S COTTAGE WITH ROUTE OF THE OLD TURNPIKE ROAD IN THE FOREGROUND.

THE OLD STONE KESH NEAR THE CLOONEEN WOOD.

THE PLACE WHERE THE TURNPIKE ROAD ONCE ENTERED THE KILLEEN ESTATE AT THE NORTHERN BOUNDARY.

CLAVINSTOWN MILL.

**THE RIVER SKANE EMERGING INTO DAYLIGHT NEAR THE
COMMUNITY SCHOOL IN DUNSHAUGLIN.**

THE NO. 13 MILESTONE AT RATH HILL LANE, DUNSHAUGLIN.

THE FORMER BLACKBULL STABLES.

THE FORMER BLACKBULL INN.

THE FORMER FLATHOUSE INN (ITS YARDS AND SHEDS WERE ONCE USED AS A TV SET FOR *THE O'RIORDANS)*, THE ROUTE OF THE OLD TURNPIKE ROAD IN FOREGROUND.

BOTH SIDES OF MILESTONE NO. 20 AT DOWDSTOWN. REMOVED IN 1962 FROM THE NEW LINE OF THE ROAD BETWEEN PHILPOTSTOWN CROSS AND KILCARN BRIDGE.

MILESTONE NO. 23 (FORMERLY NO. 24) – THE FINAL MILESTONE - AT CANNON ROW, NAVAN.

THE "SHOEING RING" STONE CIRCLE
AT DILLION'S BRIDGE SMITHY (FORGE).

These stone rings were used by blacksmiths as gauges for standardising the size of wagon wheels and forming their iron tyres, known as shoeings or rims. They normally consisted of a single circular stone or sometimes a concrete ring with a square central hole. They were often colloquially referred to as 'shoeing ring stones' or 'wheel formers'. The larger sections in the circle at Dillon's Bridge may have derived from such a stone. These large flat round stones could once be found on the sites of old forges and are often confused with millstones, but can be distinguished by the square central hole. Millstones normally have round holes in the centres, the 'runner' stones having three small rectangular slots chiselled out as drive pivots, note such on the Kilcarn millstones. The fixed or 'bedstone' had a plain circular hole in its centre. The author has heard these blacksmith's stones being described as 'shooning stones', this name possibly deriving from the Scottish word *shoon*, meaning a shoe or shoes.

DILLONS BRIDGE – BUILT IN 1860 TO CARRY THE NEW LINE OF THE TURNPIKE ROAD ACROSS THE HISTORIC RIVER GABHRA AT BLUNDELLSTOWN (IF IT SURVIVES, IT WILL BE IN THE MIDDLE OF THE M3 BLUNDELLSTOWN INTERCHANGE).

AERIAL VIEW OF DALGAN PARK, WHICH IS SITUATED WITHIN THE OLD DOWDSTOWN DEMESNE.

BRIAN BORU'S BRIDGE IN THE LIMEKILN WOOD IN DOWDSTOWN.

THE MEATH CHAMPIONSHIP MEDAL WON BY LARRY MONGEY IN 1887. LARRY WAS PLAYING FOR THE DOWDSTOWN TEAM. AS DESCRIBED IN THE BOOK, MONGEYS LIVED AT THE OLD MILL HOUSE IN UPPER KILCARN ALONG THE ROUTE OF THE TOLLROAD.

THE MARTRY MILL – THE LOCATION OF THE MILLSTONES FROM THE 'LOST' CORN MILL AT UPPER KILCARN.

MILLSTONES FROM UPPER KILCARN STORED AT MARTRY MILL.

Above is the French Burr 'runner' stone – note the angular centrifugal grooves and the circular hole in the centre. The close up shows detail of the three rectangular drive/pivot points.

Below is the French Burr bed stone. The central hole is to provide access for the drive shaft for the above runner stone.

ANOTHER PHOTOGRAPH OF THE OLD TURNPIKE ROAD, ONCE RENOWNED IN MY CHILDHOOD YEARS FOR ITS LUSCIOUS STRAWBERRY BANKS – LOOKING SOUTH FROM THE TEACHER'S COTTAGE TOWARDS TARA.